Radical Answers
from the Minor Prophets

Gary Holloway

HillCrest
PUBLISHING

Radical Answers from the Minor Prophets

HillCrest Publishing

1648 Campus Court
Abilene, TX 79601
Typesetting by Fritz Miller Studio

Printed in the United States of America

ISBN 0-89112-449-7

Library of Congress Card Number 2001088093

To Terry Briley,
my fellow worker
and the best man I know

Contents

Introduction

Perhaps you've studied the Bible all your life; to you, the Bible is a very familiar book.

But in many ways, the Bible is a strange book, no matter how long you have studied it. Particularly the Old Testament. It was written so long ago—hundreds and hundreds of years. It is written in biblical Hebrew, a language few of us speak. It is written to people who live half a world away from us. It even mentions people like "Edomites" and "Assyrians" who lived in places many of us would be hard pressed to find on a map. It speaks of nations that aren't even around anymore.

So when we come to the Bible, particularly to the Old Testament, we may have trouble realizing that this is God's word *to us*, that what the Old Testament says is relevant to our situations.

It is especially difficult in that part of the Old Testament we call "the Prophets." What is a prophet? Someone who foretells the future? Someone who lives out in the desert, wears funny clothes, and shouts at the top of his lungs?

It is most difficult to find relevancy in that part of the Old Testament known as "the Minor Prophets." We know that they are called minor prophets just because their books are shorter, but the term itself may lead us to believe they are not as important as others: "He's just a minor prophet; we don't have to pay him that much attention."

I hope this book leads you to discover one fact: there are no "minor" prophets. Any prophet that speaks from God has a message not just for his age and his world, but ours as well. I hope you discover with me just how relevant the Minor Prophets are. It's almost as if they read our morning papers. Speaking God's word to people long ago, they have an uncanny way of uncovering the hearts of those who walk our streets today.

These prophets also tear away the religious pretence they see in their day and in ours. Their message is radically counter-cultural. The old ways of living, of doing religion, of being moral will not do in the presence of a holy God. Our church and our world need to hear that shattering yet healing message.

We will not look at each Minor Prophet in detail or go through each book in its entirety. We will focus on one major theme in each of the twelve books, a theme the prophet could have ripped from today's headlines. By discovering these relevant words from long ago, we will find answers to what plagues our society and experience what God wants us to be. We will feel the power of the God who rules the nations.

One

Who is our God?

Hosea 4:1-3

"There is no faithfulness, no love,
no acknowledgement of God in the land."
Hosea 4:1

It's a famous love story. Maybe you know it. Hosea is a prophet to Israel. God tells him to marry a women who is (we'll use stronger language later) an unfaithful woman. She has the unfortunate name of Gomer, but if you can get around that, you'll get the impact of the story. She is not faithful to Hosea, and yet Hosea takes her back. He forgives her; he is faithful when she is not.

We know this is more than just a love story, a romantic story, a story of marriage between Hosea and

Gomer. This is the story of God and Israel, and (more importantly) of God and us. We serve a God who, like Hosea, takes us back, even though we have been unfaithful.

Unfaithful People

Hosea, in chapter four, makes that application both to Israel and to us. What we have in that chapter is a courtroom setting. We can think of "Perry Mason" or "Matlock" or "The Practice." We know courtroom scenes, if only through television. They also appear frequently in the Old Testament. When we think of God in a courtroom, we know that he usually plays the role of judge. The nations appear before him and he judges them in righteousness.

In Hosea chapter four, the setting is different. Here, God is not the judge but the plaintiff. It's not "Matlock," but "The People's Court." It's not criminal law, but civil. God brings a lawsuit against his people, Israel. Against us. He sues us for unfaithfulness, for non-support.

Listen to these words and see if they don't sound extremely relevant, almost contemporary:

> Hear the word of the Lord,
> you Israelites,
> because the Lord has a charge to bring
> against you who live in the land:
> "There is no faithfulness, no love,
> no acknowledgement of God in the land.
> There is only cursing, lying, and murder,
> stealing and adultery,
> they break all bounds,
> and bloodshed follows bloodshed.
> Because of this the land mourns,
> and all who live in it waste away;

> the beasts of the field and the birds of the air
> and the fish of the sea are dying."
> Hosea 4:1-3

It sounds as if Hosea has watched the evening news or read the morning paper. Doesn't this sound like the mess we are in? What's wrong with our society? There's no faithfulness or loyalty. Don't you sometimes feel that way? Some of us remember a time (it's not just a story) when people made deals involving large amounts of money with just a handshake. Once, when workers promised to be at your house to do a job, they'd actually be there. On time. You didn't even have to sign a contract.

Times have changed. Now you have to get the lawyers involved. Last week we refinanced our house. Deb and I had to sign over forty papers. Now there has to be a detailed contract for every deal because you know if you leave any kind of opening for someone to do you wrong, they will. In a heartbeat.

There doesn't seem to be much faithfulness. There doesn't seem to be much loyalty.

My dad worked for Delta Airlines for over thirty years. I can remember as a kid going to company picnics where the president of Delta greeted each employee by name. One thing Delta prided itself on for years was that they never laid off a full-time employee. They had a loyalty to their employees and, for that reason, their employees had a loyalty to the company.

Times have changed. Management and the world have changed. Delta has laid off employees just like every major company. Because of that, we don't find much loyalty in any business anymore—either from the company to the employees or from the employees to the company. We're all out for ourselves; it's the bottom line that matters.

Cursing. Lying. Murder. Bloodshed. Violence.

Read the paper, watch TV. What do we see? People do lie. Big companies lie, the government lies, and individuals lie. Even those we trust, our dearest friends, sometimes lie to us.

Bloodshed follows bloodshed. We live in a violent age, where at times (perhaps all the time) it is not safe to walk the streets. An age where kids kill kids in our schools, where traffic accidents end in shootings, where there are no safe places. Not long ago at our church, some of our women left their purses in the pews while we had our fellowship meal in another room. The front door of the church remained open. They came back to find their purses gone. We live in a time where we have to lock the church building, sometimes even when we are there.

And we wonder, "What has the world come to? Where is the faithfulness? Where is the loyalty? Why is there such lying, such hatred, such bloodshed?"

Such disloyalty even affects the physical world we live in. We are interconnected with our planet. God is the original environmentalist. He cares about the world he made. From the very beginning, he put Adam and Eve in the garden to care for it. So, we find that when we lose relationship with God, we lose relationship not just to each other, but even to the world in which we live.

Even the animals suffer. The birds of the air and the fish in the sea perish. Why are there so many endangered species today? Why do we have a land in mourning? Isn't it because we are looking out only for ourselves and we don't really care? We don't think we have a responsibility to the animals, the plants, or the earth on which we live.

Unfaithful Priests

Doesn't this sound contemporary to you? Don't you think Hosea knows us? That's the mess we're in, that's the situation in which we find ourselves. How did things get so bad? What is the root problem? Keep reading in Hosea:

> The more the priests increased,
> the more they sinned against me;
> They exchanged their Glory for something
> disgraceful.
> They feed on the sins of my people
> and relish their wickedness.
> And it will be: Like people, like priests.
> I will punish both of them for their
> ways
> and repay them for their deeds.
> They will eat but not have enough;
> they will engage in prostitution but not
> increase,
> because they have deserted the Lord to
> give themselves to prostitution.
> Hosea 4:7-10

Why are we in the mess we're in? The problem is the priests. And now you can sit back and feel good because you're not a priest. "The priest, that's the preacher," you might think. And so, you're off the hook.

But remember, as one who preaches, I am not exactly a "priest." I am no more a priest than you are as a Christian. I hope I am no less a priest than you are, since the New Testament calls all Christians "priests" (1 Peter 2:9).

So, it is here that Hosea is especially relevant. We read his words about lying, about lack of faithfulness, about violence and bloodshed and about caring for our world. We watch television and read the newspaper and say, "Isn't the world an awful place in which to live? Hasn't our culture gone bad?" We may long for the good old days that really weren't all that good.

But Hosea does not call us to nostalgia for a bygone era. Instead, he says, "The real problem is with the priests." If we are going to apply Hosea's message, we must look not only at the outside, at our culture. The real question is, "Have these attitudes invaded the priesthood, the church, God's people?"

One problem we have, which we'll never overcome until Jesus comes again, is that the church is in the world. On the night he was betrayed, Jesus said to his Father, "My prayer is not that you take them out of the world but that you protect them from the evil one" (John 17:15). Until Jesus comes, we are in this evil world.

But that's not the greatest challenge to us. That's not the real problem. The real problem is not that the church is in the world but that the world is too much in the church. The problem in Israel is that the priests were acting too much like the pagans, like the culture. Acting like the world. Do we not as God's priests, his kingdom of priests, his church, at times find ourselves acting too much like the world?

How do we do that? We don't do it on Sunday morning at church time. Well, not too much. But we leave the church building, go back into the world, go back to our jobs on Monday morning, and what do we do? We say, "The rules are different at work. You've just got to understand. Don't be naive. When you're out there in the world you have to play by the rules of the world."

And before we know it, we too, as God's people, are not faithful to others. We lack the loyalty we should have to other people. We might even find ourselves lying. We wouldn't put it that way. We're just "getting along." Just shading the truth, cutting the corners, practicing shrewd business—doing what it takes to survive in our world.

And yes, even as God's people, sometimes we can show violence. Bloodshed. Murder. If we don't literally kill others, we turn our faces when they are killed and say, "Well, that's just the way the world is. There's nothing we can do about it."

As God's people, we too can lose our sense of responsibility for the earth on which we live. We become part of a throwaway society and we really don't care, because we go to church on Sunday and we know we're God's people—God's priests.

Lack of Knowledge

What is the root problem Hosea faces—that we face? We find ourselves in a world, a culture, where there is no loyalty, where there is violence and selfishness. But we also find that the culture has invaded us. Hosea puts it this way: "My people are destroyed from lack of knowledge" (Hosea 4:6).

Now, what does that mean? Does Hosea mean the folks back then didn't know their Bibles? I don't think so. I know some use this passage to teach we really need to be in Bible classes and have personal quiet time with Scripture. We do. But for most of us, the problem is not that we don't know the Bible. It's that we don't know God.

And, strangely enough, the problem in Israel was that people could know the Bible, and quote the Bible, and yet they didn't really know God. God says in Hosea, "Because you have rejected knowledge, I also reject you as my priests" (Hosea 4:6). It's not that they were ignorant or just didn't know, that they didn't study enough. It's that they knew, yet they rejected that knowledge.

We're talking here about knowing God, not simply knowing Scripture. Now, Bible knowledge is important. That's how we come to know God. But we know that one can know all the Scriptures in the world, even memorize the whole Bible, and yet somehow not know God. The question Hosea raises, the question he wants us to ask ourselves today is, "Who is our God?" The creator, the Father of Abraham, Isaac, and Jacob—is he *really* our God? Do we know him? Is it an intimate knowledge? And how do we *know* that we know God?

Here's how we know: do we love those around us? Do we love even our enemies? Do we repay with violence those who are violent against us? That's how we really show we know God.

Are we people who are loyal, loyal to those around us, even when they are disloyal to us? Are we faithful to those around us?

What happens when we forget our God? What happens when we reject knowledge of God? We come to church and we think we know God. Yes, we praise him and we call his name and we even study our Bibles. But we don't let him completely control our lives.

Forgetting God

Here's what happens when we forget God:

> They consult a wooden idol
>   and are answered by a stick of wood.
> A spirit of prostitution leads them astray;
>   they are unfaithful to their God.
> They sacrifice on the mountaintops and
>   burn offerings on the hills,
>   under oak, poplar, and terebinth,
>   where the shade is pleasant.

> Therefore your daughters turn to
> prostitution
> and your daughters-in-law to adultery.
> I will not punish your daughters when they
> turn to prostitution,
> nor your daughters-in-law when they
> commit adultery,
> because the men themselves consort with
> harlots
> and sacrifice with shrine prostitutes—
> a people without understanding will
> come to ruin.
> Hosea 4:14

What happens when we reject God's exclusive claim on us? We start serving other gods. But surely, this part of Hosea isn't relevant to us. It refers only to that ancient world where they literally met under trees and worshipped idols.

But it is a word to us—when we forget who God is. When we forget what it means to serve God alone, when we forget loyalty, faithfulness, and love, then we are doing precisely what Israel did. We are making other gods.

What are the gods of our age? We could name several. But at least one is hinted at in this passage. It's a god who's been around a long time. Hosea says God's people go up and make their offerings to other gods under the trees "where the shade is pleasant." One god Israel was tempted to follow, and one god we are most tempted to serve in twenty-first century America, is the god of the shade. The god of comfort.

This is what we put above everything else. We Americans want our comfort. More than wanting, we think we deserve comfort. It's our right. It's not fair if we're not comfortable. Paul spoke of the gods of his day by saying, "The Jews seek a sign, and Greeks seek wisdom" (1 Corinthians 1:22). If Paul were around today, he might add, "And Americans want comfort." He does add, "But we preach Christ crucified: a stumbling block to Jews and foolishness to Gentiles." And discomfort to Americans.

Have we forgotten God? It seems like such a foolish question. We know who God is. That's why we go to church on Sunday. He's the God we worship. We know our Bibles.

But if we're not cautious, the gods of this age soon find a place beside our God. And if we are not very cautious, we can't even see the difference anymore. We want a comfortable God, a comfortable Jesus. We don't really want a God who says, "You have to be faithful and keep your word to other people, even if they cheat you." We don't want a God who says, "You have to treat the land right, because it's my world and I've given you responsibility for it." Above all, we don't want a God who says, "You have to be faithful to me, no matter what. Even if it means going to a cross and being crucified. Even if it means giving up some of your comforts—houses, cars, money, and time." We think our time is especially our own.

We want our time, our comfort. Instead, we have a God who says, "You come and follow me. I'll lead you to eternal life. But the path will go by the way of the cross."

We want a God who won't mess with us, who'll leave us alone most of the time. Who requires us to serve him a few hours on Sunday, maybe even an hour some other time in the week, but who will leave the rest of our time for us. That's not the kind of God we have. We have a God who demands all that we are.

Have we forgotten our God? We sometimes use this language about people who have quit coming to church for awhile. We say they are not "faithful" in their church attendance. But there are other ways we can be less than faithful to God. Have we forgotten God? Have we rejected knowledge? If so, we're not faithful—we are unfaithful. Unfaithful: a bland, unremarkable word. Hosea uses another word for it, a strong word. An offensive word. A word my mama told me not to use. Some versions use "prostitution," but others use an even better translation: whoredom. Hosea describes the unfaithful as "whores." It's embarrassing to say it. It should be more embarrassing to be one.

It is extremely embarrassing to act like a whore before God. Do we know what that means? This is the God who loved us. Who took us as his own when we didn't deserve it. And what have we done? We have gone to other gods: the god of comfort, the god of money, the god of getting along and being like the world. Maybe we, too, as a kingdom of priests, need to hear this indictment from God: "You have been unfaithful to me."

The God Who Forgives

That is a word of judgment. The prophets always have a word of judgment. But they always have a word of grace, also. We must always proclaim the gospel, the good news. That good news is found in both the Old Testament and the New. The gospel in Hosea, the word of grace, is this:

> Come, let us return to the Lord.
> He has torn us to pieces but he will heal us:
> he has injured us but he will bind up our wounds.
> After two days he will revive us;
> on the third day he will restore us,
> that we may live in his presence.

> Let us acknowledge the Lord;
> let us press on to acknowledge him.
> As surely as the sun rises, he will appear;
> he will come to us like the winter rains,
> like the spring rains that water the
> earth.
> Hosea 6:1-3

If we are honest, we all must admit that there are times when we have forgotten who is our God. We've gone after the gods of the age because we like the shade, the comfort. But if we will confess our unfaithfulness, if in us there is that desire to return to God each moment of each day, then there is good news. The great good news is that, yes, he is a God who judges, who wounds, but he is also a God who heals. He brings us back. Like Hosea with Gomer, God takes us back as his bride even though we don't deserve it.

The language here is significant: "After two days he will revive us; on the third day he will restore us." Raised on the third day. We can't help but think of Jesus. In Jesus, we see who our God is. He's the God who gave his only Son, the God who raised him from the dead on the third day. The one who forgives. The one who will raise us up at the last day. Even if we have been unfaithful, if we turn back to him, he is the God who raises us up with Jesus to serve him every moment of every day.

Questions for Discussion

1. Is there more lying, cheating, and violence now than there used to be, or does it just seem that way because of increasing television coverage? Give specific examples of how it is worse, better, or the same.

2. How does the land suffer as a result of unrighteousness? Does evil lead to pollution?

3. Have dishonesty and violence infiltrated the church? If so, give examples. What can we do to prevent such "worldliness"?

4. Do we suffer from lack of knowledge when it comes to God? Is it that we don't know our Bibles or that we don't do what we know to do? How can we increase our knowledge of God? How do we show we know God?

5. What are some of the "gods" of our time? Do Christians sometimes thoughtlessly follow these gods? What can we do to be faithful to the true God?

6. Does the promise of God's forgiveness tend to make us more or less faithful to him? What is the difference between forgiveness and permission?

Two

Why is God Unfair?

Habakkuk

"How long, O Lord, must I call for help,
but you do not listen?"
Habakkuk 1:2

How old were you when you first realized life was not fair?

I was about seven. At that time, my mom collected green stamps. If you're too young to remember those, stores gave them as a bonus when you shopped for groceries. You pasted the stamps in a book and then took the books to the stamp redemption center where you traded them for merchandise.

This time I went with mom to redeem the stamps.

She planned to get a toaster or a saucepan or something worthless like that (at least, worthless to my seven-year-old mind). Of course, I went and looked at the toys. I particularly noticed a toy truck, a wrecker out of blue steel with a real warning light on top. It was enough to warm the heart of any seven-year-old boy.

I wanted that truck.

But I didn't ask for it. I knew my parents loved me. They gave me all I needed. But they were good parents. They didn't give me everything I wanted.

Then the unimaginable happened. Mom must have seen the gleam in my eye. Whatever she wanted was out of stock, so she offered to trade the green stamps for the toy truck.

It was one of the greatest days of my life. I still remember riding home with that truck in my lap, overjoyed with an unexpected gift. I remember unpacking the truck from its box, playing with it, and thinking, "Life is wonderful."

Until fifteen minutes after taking it out of the box. That's when I sliced my finger deeply on the sharp edge of the metal truck. And the blood came, along with the pain. Pain always seems worse as a kid than it does as an adult. Injuries are always more traumatic. I guess after cutting your hand forty or fifty times, it's much less surprising. I remember the pain. I remember mom cleaning the wound. And I remember that I never looked at that truck quite the same way again. My joy had turned to disappointment. And I thought to myself, even at that young age, "Life is not fair."

Beyond the Sunny Side

Since then, I've come to know in even more profound ways that life is not fair. We all have. You work for months and months on that school project only to have your little brother leave it out in the rain and ruin it. And you say, "Life is not fair."

Or it happens in more severe ways as an adult. You are in the office working hard. You're in the running for a promotion. You know quite honestly that you are the best person for the job. But someone else gets the position. You find out you lost the job because the other candidate told stories behind your back, horrible rumors about you that were not true. But the damage has been done. Life is not fair.

It happens in our families. You work so hard to be a good wife, yet your husband is abusive. You know other women who don't work nearly as hard at their marriages, yet they have happy marriages. Life isn't fair. You work hard to raise your kids, do the best you can. But sometimes they still rebel against what you taught them. They turn against you, and life is not fair.

We see it in our society. A couple works four jobs between them just to put food on the family table. But they are unskilled workers. They aren't paid very much. They can't afford insurance. One of their children gets sick. Our social system will pay for basic care, but without insurance this couple cannot afford the expensive treatment needed to cure their child. The child dies, and we say, "That's not fair."

Life is not fair. We lose our children, our mothers and fathers, our husbands, and our wives to death. We see innocent children suffer through no fault of their own. We see drug dealers prosper and murderers let off scot-free. Life is not fair.

If we're Christians, we have to go one step farther. Perhaps you're offended by the title of this chapter, "Why is God Unfair?" I'm not about to stand up and say, "God is unfair." Why? Because he is God and I am not. And I am somewhat afraid of him, for good reason. He is the Almighty, the Lord of Hosts. I am but dust.

But we must all admit that God seems unfair at times. Or, at least, it seems he doesn't care that life is unfair. We wonder, "What is God doing? Why doesn't he do something about the tragedy we see in our world and in our lives? Doesn't God care?" It seems as if he doesn't.

We may react strongly to such a message. Why such pessimism? We just need to look at the sunny side of life, right? Be optimistic. Stop and smell the roses.

To others, that is an infuriating cliché. Like most easy answers, there is truth in "stop and smell the roses." God has made a beautiful world. He is a God who is wasteful in his grace. He makes his sun rise on the evil and the good. The truth is, no matter how unfair life has been, there is a joy that comes from looking at a beautiful day, smelling the roses, and counting our blessings.

What is God Doing?

But some of us have been through tragedy, and we know that there is no amount of goodness on the sunny side of life that will make up for the injustices we have suffered. The Bible does not call us to some kind of easy, empty-headed optimism. Instead, it is Scripture itself that most eloquently asks the questions, "What is God doing?", "Where is God?", and "Why does God seem unfair?"

Habakkuk asks those questions. He lives in the same time as Jeremiah, when God's people are suffering. When the innocent, particularly, are suffering. When it seems God is hiding his face and turning a blind eye to those in pain. Habakkuk does not respond by saying, "Let's be optimistic." Instead, he asks the honest and obvious question, "Where is

God?"

The oracle that Habakkuk the prophet received.

> How long, O Lord, must I call for help,
> but you do not listen?
> Or cry out to you, "Violence!"
> but you do not save.
> Why do you make me look at injustice?
> Why do you tolerate wrong?
> Destruction and violence are before me;
> there is strife, and conflict abounds.
> Therefore the law is paralyzed,
> and justice never prevails.
> The wicked hem in the righteous,
> so that justice is perverted.
> Habakkuk 1:1-4

It looks like Habakkuk watches our evening news. You know what it's like. You watch the news and the first story is of corruption in the government. Illegal fund-raising. Dirty campaign tricks. Waste of public funds. This "-gate" and that "-gate." The next story profiles a child abuser let go on a technicality. The third story is on how big business cheats the poor. And we watch with no expression on our faces. We've seen it all before. But in our saner moments we wonder, "Where is our outrage?" Have we become indifferent to injustice? Don't we care anymore?

That's what Habakkuk is asking, not of himself but of God. "God, can't you see what's happening down here? Can't you see that those who do right and work hard are sometimes victims of violence?"

We know how it is in our day. You go downtown and someone there asks you for a handout. You reach in your wallet and hand him a twenty. He grabs the wallet and runs. Is that fair? Or worse, he beats you and takes the wallet and the twenty.

Habakkuk asks, "God, don't you see the violence?

Don't you hear us crying out to you for help? Why don't you do something, God? Don't you care?"

The answer to the injustice in life is not optimism, but neither is it cynicism. Some of us have been around too long. We've seen too much. We've lost our sense of outrage. We say to those who are younger and still outraged, "What did you expect? Don't be naive. That's just the way the world works, or doesn't work. Of course the political system is corrupt. That's what politics are all about. Of course the poor are downtrodden; that's the way it's always been. Of course there are violence and injustice. You can't change it."

Is that what we do? Do we just pour out our complaint to God and not even expect God to answer? The answer of Habakkuk, the oracle he received from God, is that we should not be blind optimists but neither should we be bitter cynics. Yes, we cry out to God and say, "How long will it be before you bring justice? God, don't you see the mess we're in? Can't you see what's happening? Don't you have any feelings for us, Lord?"

God Answers Our Cries

Yet we are God's people and we expect God to answer. The good news of Habakkuk is that God will answer. Justice will come. We are not justified in being hard-hearted cynics who say, "The world's unjust and that's just the way it is."

God answers Habakkuk and us:

> Then the Lord replied:
> "Write down the revelation and make it
> plain on tablets
> so that a herald may run with it.
> For the revelation awaits an appointed
> time;

> it speaks of the end and will not prove
> false.
> Though it linger, wait for it;
> it will certainly come and will not
> delay."
> Habakkuk 2:2-3

Habakkuk looks at his age as we look at ours and we both say, "How can it be that those prosper who cheat the poor? How can it be that those who do the right thing are so many times cheated and end up on the trash heap of society?" We cry out to God and say, "How long will it be, Lord? Can't you see this?"

And the answer comes from God. He says it's a sure word. God tells Habakkuk, "Write it in big letters so no one can miss it." And here is the message: "The end is coming." That may sound like the fellow in the comics who wears the white robe and carries the huge message board saying, "The end is near!" Habakkuk means something like that. But he means more than that, more than "the end is coming, the world is coming to an end, God will make things right." He means the "end," the purpose of life, is coming. Life is not meaningless. God has an end, a purpose, a goal in mind for our lives, for our world. Even though the world is unfair, it will not always be that way.

When we look at the unfairness in the world, how do we react? We can react with sheer optimism. But that is shallow and foolish. We can be knocked out of that easy optimism by any tragedy that comes. We can react to injustice with cynicism, saying, "It's not going to get any better. That's just the way the world is." We can put more locks on our doors, get an alarm system, and stay in the house. Maybe we will be okay.

Or we can react like Habakkuk tells us to. We can react in faith:

> "See, he is puffed up;
> his desires are not upright—
> but the righteous will live by his faith."
> Habakkuk 2:4

To react with easy optimism or resigned cynicism is to be puffed up. We commit the sin of pride if we think we can make sense of the world and its injustice. No, we do not make sense, but we believe, we trust. We live by faith. "The righteous will live by faith." Paul takes this as his Old Testament memory verse. In Romans, he talks about what it means to be right with God by faith.

But what do these words mean in the context of Habakkuk? We see evil all around us. It looks as if the bad guys always win. It looks as if it does not pay to do the right thing. What do we do? Keep in mind that we live by faith. We trust. Faith and trust mean we don't live by sight. If we look out at the world, it looks as if God is not listening, evil is winning, injustice will triumph, and it just isn't fair. But if we see the world through eyes of faith and if we listen to God with the ears of faith, then we begin to see and to hear that clear message God tells Habakkuk to write, that message in large letters no one can miss. The message is that the time is coming when God will make things right. The time is coming when justice will prevail. The time is coming when the poor and downtrodden will inherit the earth. The time is coming when we who suffer unjustly will see justice done.

Wait for the Lord

If that time lingers, if it seems it will never come, what do we do? We wait on it. At the end of Habakkuk, we have an eloquent and beautiful statement of faith.

It's a reminder that our faith is not based on what we see. It's not even based on the justice of life. It may be (I pray it is the case) that you have not experienced many injustices in life. It may be that God has blessed you in so many ways. You've worked hard for a living and God has given you a good living. You've been fair and just with others and they have been fair and just with you. But my guess is that for most of you life has not worked out that way. You've been good parents and still lost your children. You've been a faithful husband or wife and still lost your marriage. You've treated people more than fairly. You've treated them not only with justice, but with generosity and mercy. And they've turned around and kicked you in the teeth. You might say, "So what's the use of being good?" If life is not fair, then why try to be good and right and just?

Habakkuk says living by faith means we stick with God even though life is unjust. At the end of Habakkuk is a beautiful poem on living by faith:

> Though the fig tree does not bud
> and there are no grapes on the vines,
> though the olive crop fails
> and the fields produce no food,
> though there are no sheep in the pen
> and no cattle in the stalls,
> yet I will rejoice in the Lord,
> I will be joyful in God my Savior.
> Habakkuk 3:17-18

I'm not sure how to modernize these sentiments. To paraphrase Habakkuk: When you're out of a job and you've searched for months and months and can't find one; when they've repossessed your house and taken away your car; when there's no food in the refrigerator; when you've run out of unemployment benefits and the governmental safety net won't catch you—even then, you'll still hang on to faith. When things are at their lowest, Habakkuk doesn't say, "Just grit your teeth and get through it." He says "Yet I will rejoice in the Lord."

We put our trust in God, believing that even though we don't see things improving and even though we suffer here, God will make things right. It may be today when he makes things right—I pray it is. Or it may be tomorrow. It may be that we don't see things made right even in our own lifetimes. We need that faith that stretches beyond our lives, that stretches to a God who is faithful and just, who sees violence and evil and injustice and who promises that, someday, he will make things right.

Waiting in Silence

What do we do in an unjust world? We trust a God who is just. In the words of the hymn "God Moves in a Mysterious Way" by William Cowper, "Judge not the Lord by feeble sense, but trust him for his grace." Or, in the often-sung words of Habakkuk 2:20: "The Lord is in his holy temple; let all the earth keep silence before him."

We sometimes sing these words to start our worship, as if to say, "It's time to be quiet now and worship God." That's not the point of the passage. The point is, in the face of injustice, what do we do? We keep silent. This does not mean the silence of apathy. No, we must lift our voices loudly against all forms of injustice. We are called to be God's people. He calls us to work for justice. To help those treated unfairly.

It's not that kind of cynical silence, but rather the silence that reminds us this is God's world, not ours. Although we work as hard as we can to help the poor, the poor will always be with us (as Jesus himself reminded us). We cannot eradicate poverty on our own. This silence reminds us that we must treat others fairly, with justice, no matter how they treat us. We work within the political system to bring in justice and fight injustice.

And yet, it's God who rules our world. The Lord is in his holy temple. He is in control, although it may not seem that way. What we are called to do is to come before him in grateful praise and even in silence. Our silence says, "God, we take this unfair world and we put it in your hands." Because, whether we put it there or not, that's where it is. The Lord is in his holy temple. Keep silence before him, because it is he who is to act.

It may be this day or this week that you are convinced again that life is unfair. One of your toys may cut you. You may not get that promotion at work, the one you think you deserve. Sickness may come upon you. A loved one may die. What do we do in the face of injustice? We don't merely put on a happy face. We don't just accept it and say that's just how life is. We fight injustice. We fight evil. But ultimately, we trust our God. We stand before him in silence. We know that he is the Lord who has promised—he's written it in big letters—that he's going to come. And he's going to make things right.

Questions for Discussion

1. Is life fair? What are some examples in your own life where it seems unfair? What would a fair life look like?

2. Are Christians supposed to be optimistic? Are cynical people more realistic than optimists?

3. In what sense do we commit the sin of pride by trying to figure out the fairness of life?

4. What does it mean in the context of Habakkuk when God says, "The just will live by faith?" Can we genuinely trust God when everything goes wrong?

5. What does it mean to keep silent in the face of injustice?

Three

Who Are We?

Amos 3:1-2

"You only have I chosen…"
Amos 3:2

Imagine someone comes into your church Sunday morning and they've never been to church before. They don't know who you are or what you do in church. They might ask the obvious question, "Who are these people?"

How would you answer? Maybe you've looked around at church at times and wondered yourself, "Who are these people?" What is it we have in common at church? I'm not sure, in a typical congregation, that we have that much in common. We are not all of the same race. We are not all male or female. We don't all support the same political party.

So I assume our answer to the question would be, "We are here because we are God's people." We might put it in other terms. We are the church. We are Christ's church, God's church, or a least that's who we want to be. We are the church of the Bible, particularly the New Testament. We could use those colorful metaphors the Bible has for the church. We are the body of Christ. As the body has many parts, all different, that work together, so we work together under Christ, the head.

The Chosen People

In the last few years the most popular term for the church is "God's family." It's a good biblical description of how we want to think of ourselves. We are the family of God. When you think of it, that's a fairly audacious thing to say. Who are these folks? We are God's family, God's children—brothers and sisters of Jesus.

How do we get to be God's family? Are we somehow naturally related to God? I don't think any of us would claim that. Instead, we are God's family because he chose us to be his children. He just reached out and picked us. Now, sometimes we talk about it differently. We invite people to come to Jesus and become part of God's family. Indeed, all of us who are children of God at one point in our lives decided to become part of his family.

Yet, more often that's not the kind of language Scripture uses to describe becoming God's children. Usually the process is described from God's point of view. It's not just that we joined up, it's that God chose us. He picked us to be his people.

So who are we? We are God's chosen people. We

are the family of God. And that gives us an amazingly rich heritage. Do you remember where that language is first used in the Bible? Go back to Genesis and you'll find the first person called by God to be his special possession, to join God's chosen people, to be the family of God. His name is Abraham.

> The Lord said to Abram, "Leave your
> country, your people, and your father's
> household and go to the land I will
> show you.
> "I will make you into a great nation and
> I will bless you;
> I will make your name great, and you
> will be a blessing.
> I will bless those who bless you,
> and whoever curses you I will curse;
> and all peoples on earth will be blessed
> through you."
> Genesis 12:1-3

God chose Abram (later called Abraham). We're not told why. Isn't that interesting? We're not told that God looked down at all the people of the earth and Abraham just seemed to be better or more faithful. We're not told why because we should see this as the sovereign choice of God. He picks who he wants to pick. He chooses Abraham. Period.

Abraham could have been disobedient to that call. He could have said, "I'd rather not. I don't want to be God's person." But he is obedient. He has faith. He trusts God. He becomes the chosen person and through Abraham we have the chosen people of God.

We usually think of the chosen people as Israel or the Jews. I don't know your family background, but most of us are not Jews by birth. We are not part of God's chosen people by physical descent from Abraham.

But if we are God's people (and that's who we claim to be), we must remember that by faith we are all Jews. We are God's chosen people. As Paul says in Romans, God took those of us who were outsiders, Gentiles, and he grafted us into that root of Judaism (Romans 11:17-21).

So, I'm proud that Abraham is my father, my ancestor. I am part of God's chosen people because by faith I come from Abraham. I think we all need to be reminded of that. "Father Abraham" is not just a strange song we sing in children's church but a fact of our faith. Through Abraham we are part of the chosen people of God that goes back thousands of years.

So who are we? We are Abrahamites. We are Israel. We are Jews. We are God's chosen people.

Our Story

You remember the history of God's chosen people. They end up as slaves in Egypt. A Pharaoh who did not know Joseph makes them groan under hard labor. Suddenly it doesn't look like a good thing to be God's family, his chosen people. To be God's chosen means to be in slavery.

But God does not forget his family. He didn't forget us. He remembered our ancestors. He sent Moses to deliver them. We all know the story of the ten plagues. With a strong hand God led his people out of slavery and brought them to Mount Sinai. There he said to them:

> "You yourselves have seen what I did to
> Egypt, and how I carried you on eagle's
> wings and brought you to myself. Now if
> you obey me fully and keep my
> covenant, then out of all the nations
> you will be my treasured possession.

> Although the whole earth is mine, you
> will be for me a kingdom of priests and
> a holy nation."
> Exodus 19:4-6

These are not just words to Israelites a long time ago. We also, by faith, are Israelites, God's people. And God says to us, "Yes, all people belong to me. I am their Creator and Lord. But by my grace I have chosen you to be my special people." If we come to him in obedience he will make us his treasured possession, a kingdom of priests who serve him.

The chosen, family language in the Old Testament is used in the New Testament about the church. Since the word "church" is used in so many ways, we might be better off answering the question, "Who are we?" by answering, "We are God's chosen." We are the people God has made his own.

Peter puts it this way:

> But you are a chosen people, a royal
> priesthood, a holy nation, a people
> belonging to God, that you may declare
> the praises of him who called you out of
> darkness into his wonderful light. Once
> you were not a people, but now you are
> the people of God; once you had not
> received mercy, but now you have
> received mercy.
> 1 Peter 2:9-10

Adopted Children

What a wonderful thing, what an unbelievable gift it is to be God's chosen people! I need to be reminded of that from time to time. My guess is that all Christians do, especially when life gets so tough. Or other times, when life seems so daily. Day follows day, things never change, and we may forget God loves us in a special way. We were no people—nobodies. We were not related to each other or to God. But God, out of his grace, has made us his people. He has blessed us beyond belief. He is not just willing to call us his people, but he even calls us his children.

> Because those who are led by the Spirit of God are sons of God. For you did not receive a spirit that makes you a slave again to fear, but you received the Spirit of sonship. And by him we cry "Abba, Father." The Spirit himself testifies with our spirit that we are God's children. Now if we are children, then we are heirs—heirs of God and co-heirs with Christ, if indeed we share with his sufferings in order that we may also share in his glory.
> Romans 8:14

The language here in Romans is that God did not give us a spirit of fear, as if we did not belong, but a spirit of adoption. God has adopted us. Adoption is intentional. When you have a natural child, one can say you made that choice. In another sense, however, you have no choice. You get the child that comes. With adoption, it's different. You choose the child. It is this child you want.

I heard recently of a family with some natural children and some adopted children. The parents made a great effort to assure the adopted children they were wanted. "You're special," they repeatedly told them. "We wanted you. We picked you out." They made such a fuss over their adopted children that the natural children became jealous. One even said, "I wish I was adopted."

All children are special. The point here is that God

adopted us when we were not his natural children. Let's be honest with ourselves. We don't naturally resemble God very much. Or as Paul says in Romans chapter eight, we are by nature "children of wrath." We deserve God's anger. But what God has done in his grace and mercy is take us as children of wrath and adopt us to be his people.

This Romans passage may mean more if we realize that adoption worked a bit differently in the New Testament world than it does in ours. In our world we usually prefer to adopt children, even infants. In the Roman world, there was the usual but cruel practice of exposing unwanted infants to the weather and letting them die. Thus there were few infants or children to adopt. The Romans did adopt adults. Remember *Ben Hur*? If you saw the movie or read the book you may remember a Roman nobleman adopted him. This was a typical practice.

Now to adopt infants or children is one thing; they're cute and can be raised the way the parents want. To adopt an adult is something else. They're already formed. They've made their mistakes and are not likely to change. You know who they are. Yet in spite of knowing who they are you adopt them. That's what God has done for us. He knew us. He picked us not because we were better looking or morally superior. We might think so, but we're fooling ourselves. No, it's while we were sinners that Christ died for us. It's while we were children of wrath, unlovable, unadoptable, that God chose us. Out of his goodness and mercy he adopted us.

Who are we? We are God's chosen people. That's not a new idea to most of us, but we need a reminder. We are, by faith, children of Abraham. For no reason at all except his sovereign choice, God picked Abraham. He made of Abraham a great nation. We are that nation. God took that nation descended from Abraham, Isaac, and Jacob, brought them out of Egypt, took them to Mt. Sinai, and there he gave them his instruction.

Why? Because he loved them. Because he cared for them. He promised them they would be a kingdom of priests. Peter says that promise comes true in Christians. We are God's people. We are that nation of priests for other people.

What a marvel it is, how wonderful it is to be God's people. We need to live each moment and take every breath with confidence that we are God's people.

The Only Chosen

All of that leads to a text from Amos. Amos, like most of the prophets, speaks to the people of God. He speaks to people like we are. People who have been chosen by God, who are God's own nation, who have been adopted by God, who are God's children. He speaks to them and to us and he says this: "You only have I chosen of all the families of the earth" (Amos 3:2).

Out of all the families, God chose us. Isn't it marvelous! Can't we be justly proud of what God has done for us? There is a good pride in the Bible, pride in the amazing mercy and grace of God.

But that good pride can easily become another kind. We can become, not proud that God in his mercy chose us, but proud that we are God's people and others are not. This seems to be Israel's attitude in Amos. They are secure in knowing they have been chosen, but they make no effort to remain close to God, to stay chosen, to keep in the path of righteousness, to fulfil the covenant they made with God.

"You only have I chosen," God says, "of all the families of the earth." Then the other shoe drops. "Therefore, I will punish you for all your sins." That's not the part of the verse we want to hear. I'm sure it's not the part they wanted to hear. What we want to hear, and what we need to hear sometimes, is "You are God's people and this is what that means." "God loves you." That's true. "You are God's special people." That's also true. "You are who you are because of what God has done." Amen. "You can be proud of who you are because of what God has done." Amen again.

But there's another side to being chosen by God. There is a responsibility in being God's family. As I said earlier, it has become popular recently to speak of the church as family. It's good biblical language and I'm all for it. But there are dangers in speaking this way. One danger is that some may have come from broken, dysfunctional, even violent families. If that is the case with you, you may say, "If the church is like a family I want no part of it."

The other danger, one I think more of us face, is when we come from good families. We hear the church is the family of God and we think we should naturally all get along and feel love for each other. We may have an ideal picture of the way our family was or is. We put that ideal picture on the church and we think family means closeness and sharing and all kinds of blessings.

But it also means responsibility. If a stranger calls me past midnight and asks for help, I hope that I'll be generous enough to wake up, get out of bed, and help them. If Dad or Mom or one of my brothers calls past midnight asking for help, I have no doubt that I will get out of bed and help them. Why? Because they're family. There is a responsibility to being family. They are the ones who have to take you in when no one else will. You have to do the same for them.

We are God's family. What does it mean? It means we have a responsibility to each other. We have to put up with one another, have patience, and care for each other, even when we don't particularly feel like it. Why? Because that's what it means to be family.

But in this passage in Amos the focus is not on our responsibility to each other but on our responsibility to God. He is the Father and we are the children. On one level, he is the giver and we are those who receive his good gifts. We did not choose him; he chose us. We did not adopt him; he adopted us. And yet, because God adopted us, because we are chosen, because we are God's people, then that's what we are expected to be. If we are God's people then we must stick to God. If God is your Father, then treat him like one.

How to Treat a Father

How should we treat a father? With proper fear, respect, love, concern, and service. What was the problem God's people had in Amos's day? They liked being God's people because it made them feel superior to others. That's one way we can misunderstand the family of God. We may get to the point where we think, "We're God's family and you're not." But part of being the family of God is to share his good news with others: the news that they, too, can be part of God's family.

The Israelites had become proud they were chosen by God. Do we ever do the same? We watch the news and read the papers. We pat ourselves on the back and say, "Boy, I'm thankful I'm not evil like those people out there." Aren't we just a little bit better, a little superior? After all, we are God's people.

So to Israel back then and to us, Amos has this brief reminder from God: "Yes, I've chosen you. But it's a great responsibility to be chosen by God. Look at

Abraham. He was chosen by God. But what does it mean? It means leaving home. Going to some new land, a land he is promised but never truly possesses. Still, he trusts God's promise. It means waiting years and years and years for God's promise of a son, until it seems impossible for it to happen. Still, he waits. And he believes. And he has that child of promise.

What does it mean to be chosen by God? For Abraham it means taking that son of promise and offering him as a sacrifice to God. And so Abraham would have done had God not stopped him at the last minute. Being chosen may cost you a son.

What does it mean to be God's chosen people? Look at Israel. Yes, they are led from Egypt. Yes, they do receive the law: all those laws about what you eat and how you eat, about how to worship, being clean and unclean. Laws that we feel really good about because we're thankful we don't have to keep them all anymore. But they are part of what it meant to be God's people. There's a responsibility about being God's people. A responsibility to God. A responsibility to be different.

There's even a responsibility for Israel and for us to be God's people for others, for the nations. God tells Israel that if they will follow him they will be a kingdom of priests, not just for their nation, but for the world. And isn't that what we are called to be? After Peter says we are a royal priesthood, he tells us to live differently from those around us. Go back to Romans. After Paul says we have been adopted as God's children he spends the rest of Romans telling us how to live as God's children. We obey the government even when it is unfair (Romans 13). We love each other with brotherly affection (Romans 12). We care for those in need.

What does it mean to be God's people?

It means God expects a little bit more from us. Don't we always expect more out of the family? We do, even though they may disappoint us sometimes. We expect more from fathers, mothers, children, brothers, and sisters.

God expects that of us.

This is not bad news. It's the greatest of news. God has chosen us as his people. He has chosen us not because we come from a certain tribe or because we are good, but solely because of his grace. But with that good news comes responsibility and a solemn warning: "You only have I known of all the families of the earth; therefore I will punish you for all your sins." We are saved solely by the marvelous grace of God. But we must not misunderstand and pervert grace. Grace does not mean that the standards are lowered for God's people. We can't say, "Yeah, we used to be legalists and take God's laws seriously but now we believe in grace and know we can get away with a bit more." Grace does not mean the bar has been lowered so we can get over it.

No, grace means we are chosen—freely chosen. It also means you are now God's man, God's woman, God's son, God's daughter. So he expects more from us as his people. But the great good news is that he also gives more. He gives us grace to follow, grace to obey, grace to be what we are: the family of God.

Questions for Discussion

1. What does it mean to be God's people? Are we proud to be God's people?

2. Does the church ever give the impression of being a closed club made up of those good enough to belong to God? Are we happy that others are not his people?

Can there be a dark side to the claim that we are children of God?

3. What are some of the responsibilities we have as God's people? What do we owe to God? To others?

4. Will God judge his people more harshly or less harshly than others? Why?

5. What is the difference between grace and permission?

Four

Are We Winners or Survivors?

Obadiah 3-4

"Though you soar like the eagle
and make your nest among the stars,
from there I will bring you down."
Obadiah 4

Are you a winner or a loser?

You may think that a silly question because you don't think in those terms. Yet in our culture winning is very important. I assume that's true in any culture. Has there ever been a society that thought, "Losing is better than winning"?

I can't remember a time when I was not competitive. Some may think competitiveness is only a male trait, but I'm not convinced that's true. I think back to the first games of my childhood, "tag" and "hide-and-go-seek." The object of the game was to not be "it." If you were "it," the object of the game was to tag or find someone else to be "it." There was some competition there.

We moved to other games around the neighborhood. If we played baseball, we wanted to win. If football, we wanted to win. If we ran a race, we wanted to win. You didn't feel good about yourself if you were picked last to be on the team or if you finished last in the race. We wanted to win, or at least not to lose.

It wasn't just games. In school, what happened on report card day? We always compared grades. We wanted to be the smartest person in the school, or smarter than our best friend, or at least smarter than someone.

You may say, "That's childhood. We're adults now and have outgrown our competitiveness." Did we? Isn't there competition as adults? Don't you want your business to succeed? Don't you want to get ahead in your career? Don't you want that promotion with its higher salary?

But isn't all this talk of winning and losing simply a display of an immature attitude? Shouldn't we want everyone to win? That sounds so good, even so pious. "We want everyone to win." The problem is it just doesn't work.

I've seen it tried at school track meets. Everyone who participates is given a ribbon. But even the youngest kids catch on this fast. They come home and their parents say, "Great, you won four ribbons." And the kid replies with a look of disappointment on his face, "Yeah, I got 'participant'" He knows who really won the races.

We all want to be winners. We even feel better, deep down, if there are losers. If everyone wins it's not quite the same.

Suppose you go to work tomorrow and receive a letter saying, "Congratulations, due to your outstanding work you will receive a 20% raise next year." You feel great. But then you learn that everyone in the company got a 20% raise. Shouldn't that make you feel better? Everyone wins! But in reality, don't you feel not quite as good as you did when you thought the big raise was just for you?

Every age has winners and losers. Why bring up the obvious? Because most churches I see in America look like congregations of winners. We have more than enough food and clothing. We have warm houses in the winter and cool houses in the summer. We drive cars that are the latest model or that at least get us where we are going. Almost all of us have jobs that pay well and are exciting—or at least tolerable. We have families with problems, but who are basically happy.

Do you still not think of yourself as a winner? Do you think, "No one really knows how tough my life is." Think again. There are thousands, even millions, of people who would gladly trade places with you.

A Word to Winners

What do you say to a church of winners? Obadiah prophesied about three thousand years ago to a nation of winners, the nation of Edom. In one brief chapter he confronts those who congratulate themselves on their good fortune. He speaks of the particular temptations that face winners.

The first temptation of a winner is pride. We think we've succeeded because we've worked a little harder or smarter than others. We're just a little bit superior.

In subtle and sometimes blatant ways we look down our noses at others, knowing that we have done better. We have succeeded where they have failed. We are winners. They are losers.

Through Obadiah, the Lord says to Edom:

> The pride of your heart has deceived you,
> you who live in the cleft of the rocks
> and make your home on the heights,
> you who say to yourself,
> "Who will bring me down to the ground?"
> Though you soar like the eagle,
> And make your nest among the stars,
> From there I will bring you down, declares the Lord.
> Obadiah 3-4

We don't like to admit it, but because we have so much going for us, we too are sometimes tempted to be proud. We think we've earned our position and are secure in it. Like the Edomites, we think we live in "the cleft of the rocks." We're secure in a fortress. No one can touch us. No one can defeat us. Nothing can stop us now.

But God says to Edom and to us, "I don't care what you think." Even if we think we are above it all, that we can soar like eagles, that nothing can touch us, God says, "I will bring you down."

There is that temptation to look down on others. We know there are poor people but they're poor because they haven't worked as hard as we have. They're poor because they lack the ability and the education we possess. Like Edom, we can look down on other nations. We are Americans who never lost a war (except for Vietnam and we haven't lost one since). We are economically superior to other nations. We even feel morally superior to them.

It can even happen in the church. In Christ we are winners. But we can easily pervert that into thinking we are superior to the evil sinners "out there" in the world. We can think we are winners in Christ through our own choice and effort.

So winners need a reminder. If we're successful, it's not simply because we're smarter or wiser or harder workers than others (although we may be all three). Whatever has caused us to win—effort, smarts, good looks—are all gifts from God. And what God has given us he can just as easily take away. We must not get too big for our britches—too big for God.

The Problem of Pride

So, God warns Edom against pride. Elsewhere in the Old Testament, he is especially concerned about Israel's pride. They are tempted to think that just because they're God's chosen people they're superior to others. They're winners and always will be.

If you go back to Deuteronomy when Israel comes out of the wilderness, God warns them as they prepare to enter the Promised Land:

> You may say to yourself, "My power and the strength of my hands have produced this wealth for me." But remember the Lord your God, for it is he who gives you the ability to produce wealth, and so confirms his covenant, which he swore to your forefathers, as it is today.
>
> If you ever forget the Lord your God and follow other gods and worship and bow down to them, I testify against you today that you will surely be destroyed. Like the nations the Lord destroyed before you, so you will be destroyed for

> not obeying the Lord your God.
> Deuteronomy 8:17-20

What's the warning to winners? What is the word of God to us who (even though we don't want to admit it) do have wealth? What does God say to us who live in a good land? The warning is, don't think you've accomplished all this by yourself. It is God who has given us all that we are and all that we have. No matter how much we win, we are reminded that it is the Lord to whom we must be faithful.

Who were the winners in the New Testament? It's hard to imagine anyone being bigger winners than the Pharisees. Many were wealthy. They kept God's law. They particularly thought of themselves as God's chosen people. One day, Jesus told a story of a winner and a loser, a story for all of us who think ourselves superior.

> To some who were confident of their own righteousness and looked down on everybody else, Jesus told this parable: "Two men went up to the temple to pray, one a Pharisee and the other a tax collector. The Pharisee stood up and prayed about himself: 'God, I thank you that I am not like other men—robbers, evildoers, adulterers—or even like this tax collector. I fast twice a week and give a tenth of all I get.'
>
> But the tax collector stood at a distance. He would not even look up to heaven, but beat his breast and said, 'God, have mercy on me, a sinner.'
>
> I tell you that this man, rather than the other, went home justified before God. For everyone who exalts himself will be humbled, and he who humbles himself will be exalted."
> Luke 18:9-14

We all know the story. We read the story and think, "Yes, Lord, we're so thankful that we're not like this Pharisee. We're thankful that we are humble." But what do we really think when we drive through the poorer, unsafe parts of town? When we see people with very little, do we think, "I'm thankful to God that I'm not like that," or, "There but for the grace of God go I?" There is some truth in that statement. It is God who has given us all that we have. But even that can be a source of pride. We think God has given us what we have because we deserve it.

So the warning comes. We shouldn't think we are secure in our $100,000 home, or $200,000 home, or $300,000 home. We shouldn't feel secure with our mutual funds and bank accounts, thinking, "Now I'm a winner. Now I've got it made."

No. If we're not careful, if we're not faithful to God, then he will say to us as he said to Edom, "I don't care how high you think you are. I don't care how secure you think you are. I will bring you down."

As Job said, "It's the Lord who gives and the Lord who takes away." The question is, do we have enough faith to confess the last part of that verse, "Blessed be the name of the Lord" (Job 2:10)?

If we are winners, let's beware the temptation of pride.

Just a Little Bit Superior

But there's another temptation that comes to winners—a different form of pride—the temptation to look down on the losers. A little later in Obadiah, God condemns Edom for being happy when others lose.

> You should not look down on your brother
> in the day of his misfortune,

> nor rejoice over the people of Judah
> In the day of their destruction,
> Nor boast so much in the day of their
> trouble.
> You should not march through the gates of
> my people
> in the day of their disaster,
> nor look down on them in their calamity
> in the day of their disaster,
> nor seize their wealth
> in the day of their disaster.
> You should not wait at the crossroads to
> cut down their fugitives,
> Nor hand over their survivors in the day of
> their trouble.
> Obadiah 12-14

The Edomites were winners who particularly enjoyed crushing the losers. When Jerusalem is sacked and the people of Judah are carried off, the Edomites stand by and clap and cheer. What's more, they do nothing to help God's people. They even take the spoils, the loot. They rejoice.

We read this and say, "That's terrible. We can't relate to this. We aren't the kind of people who gloat when bad things happen to others."

Aren't we?

The fellow next door works for another company in the same business as you. He leans across the fence and tells you his good news. He's been promoted to president of his company at twice the salary. What's more, his wife has won the magazine company sweepstakes, $100,000 per year for the rest of her life. Their daughter has been given a full scholarship to Harvard. You can see his son's new Porsche in the driveway.

What do you say to him? "That's great! That's wonderful!" Or do you, at least somewhere, harbor the wish that a car would jump the curb and ruin the Porsche? Or better, that a car will jump the curb and come straight for your neighbor so you can snatch him away at the last minute, save his life, and still be able to feel a little superior to him.

What puts such strange thoughts into our heads? If we're honest, don't we have to admit that we secretly gloat when bad things happen to others? Or at least we fail to completely rejoice with others over good fortune, particularly when we feel they don't deserve such blessings.

Maybe we're such good Christians that we don't gloat over the misfortunes of others, but we do what these Edomites did so long ago. We stand aloof from the problems of others. When things go bad for other people, do we stand aside and do nothing? We don't hurt them. We mean them no harm; we just mind our own business. What can we do to help them?

You remember another story Jesus told, the parable of the Good Samaritan (Luke 10:25-37). The priest and the Levite do nothing to harm the man. They don't rejoice in his misfortune. They simply pass by. Or in Matthew 25, where Jesus describes the judgment, separating sheep from goats. What makes one a sheep? Feeding the hungry, giving drink to the thirsty, helping the stranger, and clothing the needy. What terrible thing did the goats do to deserve the eternal fire prepared for the devil and his angels? Did they gloat over the misfortune of others? No. They did nothing. They saw those in need, and did nothing.

What's the great temptation of a winner? It's the urge to just enjoy it. We enjoy our success. It's not that we want others to fail. It's not that we are cruel. We wouldn't think of hurting someone with our wealth and power. We just leave them alone and hope they do the same to us. We are just apathetic. We take the good

God has given us and do nothing with it. Nothing. Nothing to feed the hungry, help the stranger, clothe the needy, and heal the sick.

And like the goats we are, at the judgement we hear, "Depart from me." Why? Because we're winners? No. God made us that way. But because we took his gifts, thought we were secure, and did nothing.

A Word to Survivors

We've heard the word to winners. But perhaps because of what we've been through this week, or this month, or even for years, we don't feel much like winners. Yet we don't think (or like to think) of ourselves as losers, either. Maybe the best we can say for ourselves is that we are survivors. We've been through all that life has thrown at us—loss of job, loss of health, loss of loved ones—and by the grace of God we have survived.

Obadiah has more than a word of judgment on the winners. He has a word of grace to survivors:

> This company of Israelite exiles who are in
> Canaan
> will possess the land as far as
> Zarephath;
> the exiles from Jerusalem who are in
> Sepharad
> will possess the towns of the Negev.
> Deliverers will go up on Mount Zion
> to govern the mountains of Esau.
> And the kingdom will be the Lord's.
> Obadiah 20-21

This all sounds like ancient real estate jargon that we can't understand. But these words have great meaning for us. Those who survive God's judgment will be winners. The day is coming. You can't even imagine how great it will be. The temple will be restored. We will go to Mount Zion to worship. And the greatest words to those of us who are simply survivors: the kingdom shall be the Lord's.

This is a promise to Israel that came true. The temple *was* rebuilt. They served the Lord again. The kingdom *was* restored. It's also a promise to us that *will* come true. If our faith survives, we *will* see the New Jerusalem descend from heaven. God himself *will* be the temple. We *will* see him face to face. Every knee *will* bow and every tongue confess. The kingdom will be the Lord's.

In that one phrase we find the key to winning, losing, and being God's people. Winning is an illusion. We shouldn't be proud as winners. It's simply a gift of God that he might easily take away. Losing is also an imposter. If we trust in God, no matter what happens to us, we cannot be truly losers. And if we merely survive, the great good news—whether we are winners, losers, or survivors—is not about us, anyway. The kingdom will not be ours, nor will it belong to others. The kingdom will be the Lord's.

And that's the best possible news. Our relationship to God, our ultimate existence, even our winning, is not up to us but up to God. If it seems some days like it's our world, we need to be reminded it is not. It's our Father's world. If it feels some days like it's not our world at all, that we have completely lost, we must remember that it's our Father's world.

If he is truly our Father and truly our Lord, then the question is not, "Are we winners? Or losers? Or survivors?" but "Are we faithful to our Father?" If we are, then the day will come when we can say what our Father owns, we own. Then we will be winners, because we serve the true Owner of all.

The kingdom will be the Lord's.

Questions for Discussion

1. How do adults keep score in life? Is being a winner important to you? Do we instill the will to win in our children? Should we?

2. What are the particular temptations that winners face?

3. What can we do to fight the pride we sometimes feel in our accomplishments? Is that pride always wrong?

4. Do you ever feel like a survivor? What does God promise to survivors?

5. In our winning and losing, do we ever forget who is in charge? What does it mean to say, "The kingdom shall be the Lord's"?

Five

Should We Be Angry at Evil?

Nahum 1:2-11

"The Lord is slow to anger and great in power;
the Lord will not leave the guilty unpunished."
Nahum 1: 3

We are angry. As Christians living in the twenty-first century, we are angry because things are not the way they are supposed to be. Perhaps the anger starts small. We are annoyed that we work hard to make money to pay our taxes; yet when we start to fill out the tax forms, they're so complicated we can't do it without help. We call the I.R.S. only to find out that they don't guarantee their own advice on filling out the forms. We have to spend more of our hard-earned money to pay a professional accountant to decipher the forms. That's just not right.

Our anger grows when we think of how our tax money is spent. The welfare system makes us doubly angry. It's not right when many working families don't get the assistance they deserve. It's not right when those who can but refuse to work get welfare. We grow angry at our government's lack of priorities. A recent bumper sticker: "Won't it be great when millions more are earmarked for education and we have to have a bake sale to raise money for the new professional football stadium?"

Political candidates know how to tap into our anger. Every two years, near election time, they address our anger and promise to change things. Yet it seems with few exceptions that when those candidates are elected they spend most of their time and energy getting re-elected. They forget to deliver on those promises of change. That might even make us angry enough to vote in a new bunch every two years.

Angry at Evil

If you read the papers and watch the news, the anger grows. It's not just the government that's corrupt; it's our whole society. Parents neglect their children. They leave them home unattended. They leave them in the hot car unattended. Some kids even die. Worse than neglect is intentional abuse. We see stories every day of those who rob, maim, rape, and murder. Stories of hijackers and bombers who destroy the innocent, not just in some far-way country but here at home.

We see those stories and we get angry. Or, what's worse, we've seen them so often we no longer feel anything. The most frightening thing about our society is that we are losing the ability to get angry at injustice and evil. We see so many stories we become complacent and apathetic and say, "That's just the way it is."

On those occasions when someone is caught for a crime, found guilty at trial, and sentenced to prison, isn't there something inside us that says, "Good. They got what's coming to them"? And if the crime is heinous enough—a terrorist killing, serial murders, or butchering a child—and if the criminal lives in a state with capital punishment, then even when the lethal injection is given, you say, "Good. That's right. They got what they deserved."

Do you ever feel that way? Do you feel that way, even as a Christian? Then, do you catch yourself and say, "I shouldn't feel that way; I'm a Christian"? Didn't Jesus teach us to love our enemies? To turn the other cheek? Didn't "God so love the world...?" Shouldn't we? Aren't we sinners as much as these people who committed these horrible crimes? Shouldn't we have the heart of God? Shouldn't we forgive like Jesus does? After all, we follow a loving and forgiving God, the God who forgives even us.

I ask those questions. Are those feelings—of anger, of justice, of people getting what's coming to them—are those feelings right? Is that the way God feels?

A God Slow to Anger

Nahum has something to say on how God feels about evil. "The Lord is slow to anger" (Nahum 1:3). We read those words and other passages about God and his love and realize our feelings are not always right. We need to be slower to anger. But if we read the rest of Nahum we find that slow to anger is different than no anger at all. The clear message of Nahum and the rest of the Bible is that God is angry at evil.

The anger we feel when we see injustice, when we see the innocent suffer, when we see the guilty go free, that kind of anger can be a righteous anger. It's just a glimpse of how God feels.

In Nahum those who are about to feel the anger of God against them are from Nineveh. We remember the people of Nineveh from the Jonah story. Jonah doesn't want to go to Nineveh, he tries to run away, but eventually he goes and tells Nineveh to repent. They do, which makes Jonah angry and God happy. God is always happy when people turn back to him. The righteous anger we want to have always wants sinners to repent. If we say, "They're getting what's coming to them and I hope to God they don't repent," then we've misused the name of the Lord. That's an evil attitude, not the heart of God. He always wants repentance so he can forgive. So should we.

There's a world of difference between Nineveh in Jonah's time and about a hundred and fifty years later. By then the people of Nineveh were violent people who shed the blood of the innocent. God had warned them, given them numerous chances, and they refused to turn back to him.

So God is angry.

> The Lord is a jealous and avenging God;
> The Lord takes vengeance and is filled with wrath.
> The Lord takes vengeance on his foes
> and maintains his wrath against his enemies.
> The Lord is slow to anger and great in power;
> The Lord will not leave the guilty unpunished.

> The mountains quake before him and the
> hills melt away.
> The earth trembles at his presence,
> the world and all who live in it.
> Who can withstand his indignation?
> Who can endure his fierce anger?
> His wrath is poured out like fire;
> the rocks are shattered before him.
> Nahum 1: 2-3, 5-6

This is the God who is a holy, raging fire. This is the God who takes vengeance. He sends the earthquakes, burns up the hills, and shatters the rocks. He is one angry God.

When we read this passage (which happens infrequently since Nahum is probably no one's favorite Bible book), or passages like it, we may be tempted to say, "Whew, I'm glad that's the Old Testament." We know the Old Testament God was a punishing, vengeful God, but now we live under the gospel of love. God used to be like that but we're thankful he's not that way anymore.

Wrong! There is no other way to put it. The God of the Old Testament is the God of the New Testament. Our God does not change his character. He did not suddenly become nice. He is the God of grace and love in the Old Testament, and he is the God of grace and love in the New. He is the God of vengeance against evil in the Old Testament, and he is the God of vengeance against evil in the New.

We cannot simply dismiss passages like this one in Nahum. God is a God of wrath. Why don't we want to admit that? Maybe we have good reasons, or bad ones. Perhaps we don't want to think of our God as a God of wrath because he might just direct some of it our way. And we know we deserve it; he is a holy God and we are unholy people.

But the good news is that God has turned his wrath. He's turned it from us who deserve it and placed it on Jesus. So, as people saved by Christ, we are not to be afraid of God's anger. But the truth remains that for those who refuse to be saved by Jesus, God is the God of wrath, vengeance, and indignation.

Righteous Vengeance

If that's not strong enough, later in the book of Nahum it's clear God has good reason to be angry at Nineveh. The people of Nineveh, the capital of Assyria, were not just naughty. They didn't just slip up from time to time. They were bloodthirsty people who looted the poor and killed the innocent simply to fulfil their own cruelty. Nahum has this description of God's just punishment upon them:

> O king of Assyria, your shepherds slumber;
> Your nobles lie down to rest.
> Your people are scattered on the mountains
> with no one to gather them.
> Nothing can heal your wound;
> Your injury is fatal.
> Everyone who hears the news about you
> Claps his hands at your fall,
> For who has not felt your endless cruelty?
> Nahum 3:18-19

The punishment is described this way: they are led out as captives; their wound is mortal; they're going to be destroyed. And as they are led in defeat past the other nations, those nations clap and cheer.

We may be uncomfortable with that last phrase, but we need to remember this is not what we saw condemned in the previous chapter. This clapping and cheering does not come from an ungodly feeling of superiority to others. It's not rejoicing over the pain of others because we are glad it didn't happen to us. We're not talking about the attitude of Jonah, who wants people not to repent. We're talking here about the attitude of God. Sometimes people do get what's coming to them and it's a good thing. The word for that is justice. When the wicked and violent get what's coming to them, it is right. It is just. It's the way it should be. And we should clap and cheer.

How far do we take that? I don't have all the answers about capital punishment. I'm not convinced that our justice system is completely fair. To avoid even the possibility of executing the innocent, perhaps capital punishment should be outlawed. Those who favor capital punishment are sometimes asked, "Yes, but could you throw the switch?"

It's not a fair question. What we're talking about here is not a personal vengeance, but justice and righteousness. It's the vengeance of God. We must understand that we are not operating from a personal hatred of the criminal, and that God does not hate the sinner. As hard as it is to understand, vengeance is part of God's love. With that in mind, maybe we could throw the switch or at least admit it is right for someone to throw it.

If this kind of talk sounds completely contrary to Christian love, we must remember God's wrath is found in the New Testament as well as in the Old. Who is it that goes into the temple area and violently scatters the tables and the money? Who makes a whip and "drives them out" ("them" being the cattle and perhaps even the moneychangers)? And why does he drive them out? They have made the temple a den of thieves. They have offended the holy God. Doesn't Jesus show the character of God when he himself acts as the holy, vengeful God?

Jesus shows righteous indignation. Isn't he our example? Don't we sing songs about wanting to be like Jesus? Do we want to be like the real Jesus revealed in the gospels or like the Jesus of our imaginations—the meek, mild, never-hurt-a-fly Jesus?

But we must be careful. Our problem (or at least, my problem) is we're not sure whether or not our anger is righteous. Do we crave justice or are we merely irritated? Is it God's righteousness or personal vengeance we seek?

Apathy at Evil?

Our greatest temptation may not be toward unrighteous indignation but toward no indignation at all. We are apathetic. We excuse injustice by thinking, "That's just the way the world is." Obviously, if we are for evil, that's wrong. But I don't think many of us are going to clap and cheer for the bad guys. But we might stand on the sidelines and not do anything.

Jesus wasn't apathetic about evil. When the disciples saw him cleanse the temple, they remembered the verse, "Zeal for your house has eaten me up." Are we eaten up with zeal against evil?

Look at Jesus again, this time in the book of Revelation. As the Lamb of God he opens the seals of the scroll of God's vengeance.

> When he opened the fifth seal, I saw under the altar the souls of those who had been slain because of the word of God and the testimony they had maintained. They called out in a loud voice, "How long, Sovereign Lord, holy, and true, until you judge the inhabitants of the earth and avenge our blood?" Then each of them was given a

> white robe, and they were told to wait a
> little longer, until the number of their
> fellow servants and brothers who were
> to be killed was completed.
> Revelation 6:9-11

The picture is clear. Under the throne of God are the martyrs. Is there any greater example of what it means to be Christ to others? Perhaps we ask ourselves, "Would I have the courage to give my life for Christ?" These Christians did. We have to admire their example.

What do these martyrs do? They cry for vengeance. "How long until judgment and vengeance?" they cry. Are we more spiritual than these martyrs? Are they simply bloodthirsty? No. They want vengeance but they didn't take personal vengeance. They turned the other cheek until they died. Like Jesus, like Stephen the first martyr, they no doubt prayed, "Father, forgive them."

But that doesn't mean they thought what happened to them was okay. What they had experienced was unjust. That made them angry—rightfully so, righteously so. Thus they do not take revenge themselves, but they cry out to the God of vengeance. And they say, "How long?"

I think we need more of that spirit of the martyrs. What we need in the church is more anger. Perhaps we have grown too apathetic toward the evil we see. Don't misunderstand. It's natural to mistrust our feelings here. Personal vengeance is always condemned. That's not God's kind of anger. If someone strikes us on the right cheek, what do we do? We turn the other one. If someone cheats us, takes advantage of us, steals our coats, what do we do? We give then the shirts off our backs. If we are forced by the government to go a mile (and we all have gone a mile out of our way because of government bureaucracy), what do we do? We go two. That's the attitude of Jesus, the attitude we must have.

How do we treat those who are unjust and violent? We love them. But what does it mean to love them? It means we want what is best for them. And what is best for murderers, child abusers, and other violent criminals? Two answers. What is absolutely best for them is turning back to God. Deep down we want most for them to repent and be forgiven. But what is best for them if they will not turn to God, maybe even best if they do? What's best for them is justice and punishment.

Not Acceptance But Forgiveness

Still, we are uncomfortable with justice and punishment. We still sing the old hymn, "Just as I Am," and we want God to take us as we are. We even (in our best moments) want God to take murderers and rapists and those who cheat the poor just as they are. But what does that really mean? God accepts us just as we are but only if we are willing to come to him, only if we are willing to be changed by him.

Do we really want God to accept murderers exactly as they are? With no remorse? With no guilt? With no will to change? I don't think so. We want them to repent. That correct desire for grace can be twisted into accepting what is evil. God cannot do that. He cannot be an evil God who approves or ignores sin. Our God is love, but our God is holy. He will not accept what is evil. He will forgive it, but forgiveness is not the same thing as acceptance.

Grace does not mean we turn a blind eye. Grace is not the same thing as leniency. We want mercy from God, but mercy is not indulgence. We know this with our own children. We love our children, love them more than our own lives. As parents, we want to show grace and mercy to our children. But are we good fathers and mothers if we let our children get away with anything? If we ignore their faults and never discipline, is that love? Is it grace? Is it mercy? Is it a compliment to say about a mother, "She lets her kids do anything they want"? Or about a father, "He never said 'no' to his children"?

In the same way, we should not want criminals to get away with it. God does not want evil people to get away with it. The best thing for them, as well as for us, is to come and to turn and to be forgiven. So in the middle of all the language about vengeance in Nahum, there is a word of grace for those who will turn to God.

> The Lord is good, a refuge in times of
> trouble.
> He cares for those who trust in him,
> Nahum 1:7

Our God is a consuming fire, a God of wrath against evil. Yet he is good. Our childhood prayers are right: God is great, God is good. But to whom is he good? He is good to those who look to him for protection. He's a stronghold for those in trouble.

There's a difference between good people and bad people. That's obvious even to the youngest child. But over and over again in our culture we are told there is no difference. That those who work hard at their jobs, pay their taxes, and care for others are no better than those who kill and maim and abuse. We're all pretty much the same.

If we mean by that that we are all sinners, that's true. We are all the same. None of us deserves the grace of God. But there is a difference between good people and evil people. It isn't some innate difference in ourselves that we can be proud of. The difference is, good people are those who seek a refuge in God, those who turn to God. If we turn to him, he will protect us. He is stronger than anything that confronts us. He's stronger than any injustice we will go through.

But to those who refuse to turn to God, the good news (and I think it is good news) is that God will not let them get away with it. We are right to be angry at evil. We hate the sin and love the sinner. But if we really love the sinner we don't want her to get away with her sin. We want her to turn and receive grace, mercy, and forgiveness.

Nahum is thus meant to be an encouraging word. It may not look that way at first, for it doesn't look like bad people get what's coming to them. It might look like they get away with it and even prosper. But the time will come when the God of wrath will take his vengeance. The time will come when justice is done. The time will come when God takes the good people, those who flee to him for refuge, to be with him forever.

We pray it's soon.

Questions for Discussion

1. What in our society makes you angry?

2. Are we ever right in rejoicing when evil is punished? Is vengeance a bad thing?

3. Is God an angry God? Do we like to think of him that way? What would it be like if God were never angry at evil?

4. What about capital punishment? Should Christians support it? Should they be against it? Can we disagree on this and still be brothers and sisters?

5. Will God forgive those who do not repent and who persist in their sin? Do we want God to forgive them if they will not repent?

Six

Will God Save Just Anybody?

Jonah 3:10-4:5

"When God saw what they did
and how they turned from their evil ways,
he had compassion and did not bring upon them
the destruction he had threatened."
Jonah 3:10

Who makes you angry?

Nahum teaches us that it is right to be angry at evil. We serve a God who is angry at evil. In the Book of Nahum, God is particularly angry at the violence and bloodshed produced by the people of Nineveh. At the end of his book, Nahum pictures God's people as even clapping and cheering when Nineveh gets what's coming to them.

What group makes us angry enough to clap and cheer as we witness their destruction? We don't get worked up about Nineveh, but perhaps we all have particular people who anger us with a righteous indignation. Who is it that makes us cry out (in the words of Scripture), "How long, O Lord? How long will you allow these people to do what they do and get away with it?"

For some of us, it's the violent who make us angry. How can God turn a blind eye to drive-by shooters who kill the innocent? How can he stand by when a terrorist detonates a truck full of explosives, killing hundreds—including small babies? Surely our God hates violence. It makes him angry.

For others of us, the freeloaders in our society make us angry. They're healthy, they could get a job; but they refuse, out of laziness. They prefer to prey off the innocent by begging, stealing, or fooling them into giving their money. They refuse to support themselves. Doesn't that make God angry?

All of us get angry with anyone who would harm a child. Our fists clinch in rage at parents who neglect their own children. Worse are those who physically abuse children. How long will it be until God punishes the child molesters? How can he stand by when some sell drugs to children to enslave them?

Perhaps we get angry with the militant homosexuals in our society. I'm not talking about those who struggle with homosexual temptation, but those who are blatant about their right to practice any form of homosexuality. They say, "This is my lifestyle. You have no right to judge me." They call us evil, narrow-minded, and homophobic if we object (or imply God objects) in any way to what they do.

Who is your Nineveh? Who burns you up? Who do

you want God to punish because they deserve punishment?

A Reluctant Prophet

Two books before Nahum in the Old Testament, about 150 years earlier, Nineveh was still around. The city was just as evil then as it was in Nahum's day. And Nineveh really burned up a man named Jonah. To Jonah, the people of Nineveh were the epitome, the model of what we should not be. They lied, cheated, stole, and harmed the innocent. They were violent people, murderers.

So God, who has a strange sense of humor, came to Jonah. He said, "Jonah, I want you to be my prophet. I want you to go and speak the word I will give you. I want you to go to Nineveh and warn them to repent and then come back to me."

We all know the story. But let's play a little game, a pretend game. Think of that group whose actions make you angry. It may be one we mentioned above. It may be another. Think of the people who burn you up, the ones you'd most want to get what's coming to them. Or maybe think of a national group or a racial group you don't really care for. What if God asked you to be the preacher, the prophet to the child-molesters or the murderers or the drug pushers? Your job is to tell them, "God wants to forgive you. He wants you to come to him and repent."

Would you hear that call? Would you preach to them with enthusiasm? Or would you be reluctant to go? We know what Jonah does. He's told to go to Nineveh and instead he gets on a ship to go in the opposite direction. This is the story we all learned as kids—ship, storm, overboard, whale, shore. Jonah is the whale book ("Whale did swallow Jo-Jo-Jonah").

That's the part every child knows.

A Gracious God

But that's really not the point of Jonah. It's not the whale book. It's not really even the Jonah book. Jonah is not the main character of the book—God is. The Book of Jonah is the story of a God who is so gracious that it is offensive. You remember that after the whale episode, Jonah goes to Nineveh and preaches, telling them to repent or perish. They repent. God takes away their punishment. How does Jonah react?

> But Jonah was greatly displeased and became angry. He prayed to the Lord, "O Lord, is this not what I said when I was still at home? This is why I was so quick to flee to Tarshish. I knew that you were a gracious and compassionate God, slow to anger and abounding in love, a God who relents from sending calamity. Now, O Lord, take away my life, for it is better for me to die than to live."
> Jonah 4:1

We hear missionary stories and perhaps we all think how great it would be to be a missionary. How wonderful to tell the good news to people and have them come back to the Lord. But what if you were a missionary to that group you despised and detested? That's the way it was with Jonah. He's the most successful missionary of all time; the whole city repents, but he's angry about it. He didn't want to be successful.

So Jonah prays to die. It's an interesting prayer. In it we have a refrain echoed throughout the Old Testament: "You are a gracious and compassionate

God, slow to anger and abounding in love." In the rest of the Old Testament, it is a profound statement of praise to the God of grace. When we read those words, we usually think, "Yes! That's the kind of God we want, one who will be gracious and forgiving."

But if we look deep within our hearts, we must admit we want that kind of God *for us*. We want him to forgive us. We don't always want him to forgive others: not the rapists, not the murderers, not the child abusers. We don't want him to be that kind, compassionate God for them.

That's the problem with Jonah. He wanted a slow-to-anger God when it came to his sins or to Israel's sins. But look what God has done now. God has been gracious to a bunch of Ninevites. Jonah says, "I knew this would happen." His words about the compassionate God are not words of praise but of blame. He has the same refrain every parent has heard: "It's not fair!" God, the problem with you is that you are not a fair God. You're a gracious God—gracious even to Nineveh.

An Angry Prophet

So, like a spoiled child, Jonah is so angry he says, "I just want to die." If Jonah cannot get his way, he will simply check out and wash his hands of God and Nineveh.

> But the Lord replied, "Have you any right
> to be angry?"
> Jonah went out and sat down at a place
> east of the city. There he made himself
> a shelter, sat in its shade and waited to
> see what would happen to the city.
> Jonah 4:4-5

Jonah thinks, "Maybe it's not over. You know how those Ninevites are. Perhaps they'll return to their wicked ways and God will punish them after all." So Jonah decides to wait awhile and watch these Ninevites. God works to make his wait more comfortable.

> Then the Lord God provided a vine and made it grow up over Jonah to give shade for his head to ease his discomfort, and Jonah was very happy about the vine. But at dawn the next day God provided a worm, which chewed the vine so it withered. When the sun rose, God provided a scorching east wind, and the sun blazed on Jonah's head so that he grew faint. He wanted to die and said, "It would be better for me to die than to live."
> Jonah 4:6-8

I lived for seven years in Texas. When it hits 107 degrees day after day after day, you'd give most anything for a little shade. I think I know how Jonah feels. Jonah's really happy about the shade. Until God takes the shade away and Jonah again says, "Just let me die."

Which leads to the point of the Book of Jonah.

> But God said to Jonah, "Do you have a right to be angry about the vine?"
> "I do," he said. "I am angry enough to die."
> Jonah 4:9

Jonah is one angry prophet. He's mad at Nineveh and they deserve it. He's also mad at God, because God's not fair. Then he gets mad about the vine. God gave it then he took it away. Everything makes Jonah angry.

Everything except...

> But the Lord said, "You have been concerned about this vine, though you did not tend it or make it grow. It sprang up overnight and died overnight. But Nineveh has more than a hundred and twenty thousand people who cannot tell their right hand from their left, and many cattle as well. Should I not be concerned about that great city?"
> Jonah 4:10-11

That's a strange way to end the book, but that's how Jonah ends. God says, "Look, Jonah, you're angry about the wrong thing. You should be angry, but not at Nineveh, not at the people, but at the evil they do." If we are genuinely angry at evil, not at people, then shouldn't we be happy when they repent? We should rejoice over a gracious God and over all who come to him in repentance. Jonah is more upset about a vine than he is concerned about the eternal well-being of an entire city.

Still, A Gracious God

So the question of the Book of Jonah is a question we might ask. Does God save just anybody? Even the worst people we know? Isn't it true that God is going to save the good folks? Oh, not the perfect—nobody's perfect—but those like us who are basically good?

And the answer of the Bible, the really offensive answer, is that God is a gracious, slow-to-anger God who will save just anybody. No matter how bad they are. No matter what they've done. God will save drug pushers who prey on children. He'll save rapists and child molesters and those who plant bombs. He will even save those in the church who may be hypocritical at times. God is so merciful, he may even save upper-middle class, respectable Americans who have large houses and cars and let other people starve.

"Oh, no, he won't," we think. Sure, God is merciful, but only to those who somewhat deserve it. Only to folks like us. But God tells Jonah that even the worst of people, if they will turn to God (that's all it takes), will find full forgiveness and salvation.

Perhaps, like Jonah, we think that's not quite fair. Aren't we somewhat suspicious of jailhouse conversions and deathbed confessions? Is it fair for us to serve Jesus all our lives and give up the pleasures of the world for him, only to find that a terrible, hateful, violent, and cruel man can turn to God at the end of his life and God will save him?

But God saved Nineveh. And if we go to the New Testament, it's even worse. Jesus tells stories of God saving pretty much anybody. Anybody who will turn to him. In Matthew 20, Jesus tells the story of a man who needed some day laborers in his vineyard. So, early in the morning, he drove the ancient equivalent of a pickup truck to the street corner where the day laborers gathered and hired a few, promising to pay them a fair day's wage. Three hours later, around 9 AM, he needed more men, so he found some and promised to pay what was fair. The same at noon and three PM. He even went out an hour before dark and hired some more.

At the end of the day it was pay time. The owner paid those who had worked one hour a full day's wage! The ones who had worked all day started grinning and nudging one another, thinking, "This is great! If they got a day's wage for one hour, we should get ten or twelve days of pay!" But the owner paid them only one day's wage. Not fair!

> When they received it, they began to grumble against the landowner. "These who were hired last worked only one hour," they said, "and you have made them equal to us who have borne the burden of the work and the heat of the day."
>
> But he answered one of them, "Friend, I am not being unfair to you. Did you not agree to work for a denarius? Take your pay and go. I want to give the man who was hired last the same as I gave you. Don't I have the right to do what I want with my own money? Or are you envious because I am generous?"
> Matthew 20:11-16

Are we like Jonah? Are we envious because God is generous? Our God is not unfair to us. He is generous. If we bask in that grace, shouldn't we want that for others, no matter how bad they are? Isn't God's grace for everyone?

For everyone? Do we really want God's grace to extend to everyone? Don't we feel comfortable with God giving his grace to us? But what about those who are worse than we are (and there are many out there who are worse than we are)? Don't we at least want them to somehow get up to speed? They should meet certain standards. They should prove they've repented. They should come to church and be good people for a while. Then, and only then—surely!—God will forgive them.

A Loving Father

Jesus told another story, perhaps his most famous,

about a bad man. An evil and ungrateful man. Maybe that's the group that really burns us up, those who receive and are ungrateful. He's a man who goes to his father and says, "Dad, I can't wait till you die. Can I have my inheritance now?" So the father gives his son the inheritance. The son wastes it all and finds himself in abject poverty. Finally he decides to go home in hope of being just a slave in his father's house.

You know the story. The father sees him coming. The father doesn't say, "Yes, be a slave for a while, prove you've really changed, and then perhaps I'll take you back." No. This father is not fair. He embraces his son, calling for robe and ring and fattened calf.

Then enters the good son. The good son is where he always is, out in the field, working for his father without being asked. He hears the party sounds and asks a servant, "What's going on?" "Your brother is home," the servant replies, "and your father has thrown a huge party." The older brother becomes angry and refuses to join the party. If he can't have his way, he will wash his hands of his father and his brother.

> So his father went out and pleaded with him. But he answered his father, "Look! All these years I've been slaving for you and never disobeyed your orders. Yet you never gave me even a young goat so I could celebrate with my friends. But when this son of yours who has squandered your property with prostitutes comes home, you kill the fattened calf for him!"
>
> "My son," the father said, "you are always with me, and everything I have is yours. But we had to celebrate and be glad, because this brother of yours was dead and is alive again; he was lost and is found."

Luke 15:28-32

Jonah. The workers in the vineyard. The prodigal. We know the stories. What do they mean for us? They are all anger stories. This anger we have at evil is right and good; we should be angry at evil. But that anger is also tricky. If we aren't very careful, we get angry, not at evil, but at people. We think if someone commits an evil act, they must be evil. That's true. But then we make the leap of thinking they are so evil they must be worse off than we are, that they are so bad they cannot come back to God.

And the story of Jonah is that God is such a gracious God he'll save just anybody, anyone who comes to him. The story of the workers in the vineyard is that God is such a gracious God that he will pay us all alike, even those who come latest to work. Those who worked hardest don't get more than others and even those who worked very little get the same. The story of the Prodigal Son—or, more properly, the story of the Loving Father—is about an older brother. A brother who, like Jonah and those first workers, has forgotten what grace means.

If we are tempted to shake our fists at God and say, "You're not fair," let's remember that's the best news of all. Yes, God is a just God who judges fairly and hates evil. But he is not a fair God, he is a gracious God. And we should want God to forgive the worst of sinners—the murderers, and rapists, and terrorists. Why? Because we want God to forgive us.

God does not grade on the curve. We dare not think that because we keep our sin rate lower than others God approves of us. How do we score on our best days? 95% righteous? 90%? Lower? Do we just hope the cut-off for salvation is lower than our grades? No. God demands complete righteousness—100%. We dare not compare ourselves to others, but to Christ.

The good news is that Christ's grade counts for us! God has opened his arms to us, paid us what we do not deserve. Saved us, Ninevites that we are.

The great, good news of Jonah is God will save just anybody. Even us. Amazing grace! We must have joy, not anger, when he offers that grace to others. We must tell that good news to the worst of sinners. God is not angry with them if they will but turn to him.

Questions for Discussion

1. What group or type of person makes you most angry? Would it make you angry if they turned to God and were forgiven?

2. Why do you think God picked Jonah to preach to Nineveh? Would we send people out as missionaries to countries they hated?

3. Why does Jonah get so angry about the vine? Do we ever let things make us so angry that we take it out on people?

4. What makes us suspicious of jailhouse conversions and deathbed confessions? Are we like those first workers in the vineyard?

5. Is God fair? Is it fair of him to forgive just anybody? Do we want him to be fair with us?

Seven

Is There Hope for Our Cities?

Zephaniah 3:1-5

"Woe to the city of oppressors,
rebellious and undefiled!"
Zephaniah 3:1

What is the biggest problem our country faces?

Several candidates come to mind, but one we all would agree on is the physical and moral decay of our cities. If you've been to some of our larger cities—New York, Chicago, Houston, Los Angeles, or Washington, D. C.—then you know what certain sections of those cities are like. They look like war zones. People live in buildings that are rubble. Many sleep on the street. The police are afraid to venture into some areas, because of snipers or drive-by shootings. There's crime, poverty, and general hopelessness.

Is there hope for our cities? Are there solutions to these intractable problems? As Americans we tend to think there is a solution to every problem. But with our cities we have tried almost everything and nothing seems to work. Some think the answer is new government programs. Others think we should just fund the programs we have. Another group thinks the solution is to dismantle the government programs we have or at least to stop funding them. Some prefer free-market solutions over government intervention. Others call for faith-based programs in the private sector.

Solutions? I'm not convinced. Still, love of neighbor prompts us to do more than feel sorry for those in our inner cities. We must do something to bring them real help. Perhaps some of us just thank God we don't live in a big city. But in truth, there is no place in left in America—country, small town, or suburb—where we can escape the problems of crime, decay, poverty, and violence. All America is urbanized. The city with its problems has come home to us all.

The Unholy City

Is there hope for our cities? What is the root problem?

The prophet Zephaniah writes to Judah and tells her what she wants to hear: all the ungodly nations around Judah will be destroyed. That sounds great until Zephaniah turns his gaze to them. God is not only talking about those bad nations or the problems in those cities. He's primarily concerned with a particular city. His city—Jerusalem. Here is the real problem of Jerusalem.

Woe to the city of oppressors,
    Rebellious and defiled!
She obeys no one,
    she accepts no correction.
She does not trust in the Lord,
    She does not draw near to her God.
    Zephaniah 3:1-2

What's the biggest problem in your city? I live in Nashville, a city of churchgoers, but the problem is the same here as in all cities, the same problem as in Jerusalem.

We have not turned to God. We have not trusted in the Lord.

I'm not implying that those who live in cities are necessarily more sinful than those in the country or in small towns. One doesn't turn away from God the moment he or she passes the city limit sign. But cities have always gotten bad press, even in the Bible. Who began the first city? It was Cain, the first murderer. "Cain was then building a city, and he named it after his first son Enoch" (Genesis 4:17). What about other biblical cities? What caused Lot's problems? He camped too close to a city, a city he later inhabited—a city named Sodom.

Sodom. Gomorrah. Tyre. Sidon. Babylon. Think of all the cities in Scripture. With few exceptions, the city was the place you went to get away from God. To go your own way.

Have things really changed? In America and in the world at large, more and more people are coming to cities. Why do people leave small towns to come to the big city? Why did those in the ancient world come to cities?

Partly out of a desire to be secure. In ancient times, cities offered protection from enemies. In cities, large numbers could band together behind thick, protective walls to fight the enemy. Actually, today we usually feel less secure in the city. We put double locks on our doors and install security systems. But many still come to the city for the promise of financial security, more opportunities, better jobs. There's nothing wrong with wanting to be secure. But we must remember that thick walls, large armies, or a robust economy never provide absolute security.

What does the city do to us? Ironically, it alienates us from others. Sure, there are more people around, but one feels more alone in the city. In the small town where everyone knows you, we can think of ourselves as a community with shared outlook and values. That's harder in the big city. You might not even know the person who lives beside you, much less on down the block. If you do get to know them, they'll probably move before long. City friendships are transient. We are a people on the go.

Some like that about the city. They move to the city to be anonymous, to get lost in the crowd. They want to get away from parental control, or the small-mindedness of a small town, or community standards. They want to be free. Perhaps they even want to get away from God.

That's the way it was in Jerusalem, according to Zephaniah. The citizens of the Holy City were rebellious, defiled, and violent. They were not holy because they rejected God. They would not take correction.

Corrupt Leaders

What was the problem in Jerusalem? The same problem we find reported in our morning papers.

> Her officials are roaring lions,
> Her rulers are evening wolves,
> who leave nothing for the morning.
> Her prophets are arrogant;
> They are treacherous men.
> Her priests profane the sanctuary
> And do violence to the law.
> Zephaniah 3:3-4.

Almost without exception, city officials become corrupt. Here they are called lions. This is not the picture of a courageous beast but of a scavenger that tears and rips his prey. We elect officials to serve us and very soon they start to serve themselves, preying on us.

The rulers, better translated "judges," are hungry wolves. Instead of giving justice to the oppressed, they sell out to the highest bidder. They wolf down the helpless. Where can the downtrodden go for justice when the justice system itself is corrupt?

Politicians take bribes. Judges, too. But what about religious leaders? Surely we can trust them. But no. The prophets are arrogant and treacherous. You really don't want a prophet who tries to fool the people. Prophets are to speak for God, not fend for themselves. A prophet who speaks for profit, who tells the powerful what they want to hear, is worse than a corrupt politician or judge. Worse, because he claims his message comes from God himself.

Even the priests, those who bring sacrifices to God on behalf of others, profane the temple and the law. They hypocritically go through the motions of religion without living for God from the heart. They preach but do not practice. Their actions cause others to ridicule God.

Does this sound like where you live? We make our homes in cities filled with violence and overwhelmed with problems. Those who promise better times—politicians, judges, and even religious leaders—are part of the problem, not the solution. We have relied on our elected officials and found the system corrupt. We have depended on the justice system and found verdicts are for sale. We have relied on religion and found the preachers hypocrites.

God in the City

What do we do? Throw our hands up in surrender and despair? Is it all bad news? To whom do we turn?

> The Lord within her is righteous;
> He does no wrong.
> Morning by morning he dispenses his
> justice,
> And every new day he does not fail,
> Yet the unrighteous know no shame.
> Zephaniah 3:5

In the middle of this long, depressing look at the corruption of the city, Zephaniah reminds us that God himself lives in the city. It's true that politicians are corrupt. We can't rely on political solutions. It's true that even the best of religious leaders are sometimes hypocritical. Even though Zephaniah prophesied during one of the greatest religious revivals among God's people—the reform of King Josiah—he knows that solutions to the problems of the city do not come from human religious leaders. They don't even come from religious rulers.

We cannot rely on politicians for solutions. They are part of the problem. We cannot rely on religion. But no matter how bad things get in the city, the good news is we can rely on a faithful God. There is hope for our cities. That hope is that we as a people, as a city, will turn back to God.

Is that a real hope? Do we really believe that everyone in New York or L.A. will suddenly become a devout Christian? That everyone in your town will turn to God? I'm not sure that will happen, but I'd like for it to happen. I pray that it happens. What if it did happen? Would all our problems be solved immediately? Would we suddenly have no poverty? Would all crime cease? I don't think so. Christians are not perfect. We bring our own problems to the city.

But such a mass conversion would take care of our biggest problem. If my city, Nashville, truly turned to God, if we left behind our façade of being religious and became genuinely holy, what a difference it would make.

God's Remnant in the City

Zephaniah does not believe that everyone in God's city, Jerusalem, will turn back to him. But here is what he does believe, what God tells him, what we hope for: that no matter how corrupt the city gets, God's people will be faithful. And that faithful remnant of God's people will be enough to preserve the city. They will be a blessing to the city.

The word of hope from Zephaniah:

> On that day you will not be put to shame
> for all the wrongs you have done to me,
> Because I will remove from this city
> those who rejoice in their pride.
> Never again will you be haughty on my
> holy hill.
> Zephaniah 3:11

Perhaps the worst problem in the city is that we

trust too much in our own solutions. We rely too much on the help of the experts, the government, and religious leaders. God says there will come a day when he does away with those who arrogantly think they have all the answers to our problems.

On that day, God will preserve our cities through a righteous remnant.

> But I will leave within you the meek and
> the humble
> who trust in the name of the Lord.
> The remnant of Israel will do no wrong;
> they will speak no lies,
> nor will deceit be found in their
> mouths.
> They will eat and lie down
> and no one will make them afraid.
> Zephaniah 3:12-13

We are afraid in our cities: afraid of violent crime, afraid of the results of poverty and decay, afraid of loneliness. Many years ago, Deb and I, along with another couple, were foolishly driving through the worst part of Washington D. C. late at night. I was afraid, because I was too foolish to know that it was the wrong part of town until I saw what was happening around me. Those gritty television cop shows don't lie. There are amazingly disgusting and frightening things that happen in our cities. I feared for my safety. It's hard to imagine what it's like to live in those places, hard to imagine the constant fear.

Even in the safe parts of the city there is fear. That's why the alarm companies call me twice a week, trying to sell me a system to make me safe. That's why there's a bolt on my door (two, actually). How can we overcome that fear? With a government program that would end injustice, poverty, and crime? With more police patrols? With stricter laws and harsher sentencing?

I don't think so. Yes, we do have a responsibility to our cities. We are called to work for justice, to fight poverty, to shelter the helpless. The law of love demands that we do what we can to end substandard housing, provide economic opportunity, and treat our neighbors (even those in the worst sections of the city) as we want to be treated. We don't solve the problems of our cities by fleeing them to the "safe" suburbs. What's more, we don't solve their problems through any human program.

So what can we do for the city? We can be God's people. We can be what God calls a holy remnant. We can be those who do no wrong, who do not lie or deceive. We can be meek and humble in the midst of the city. We can put God first. We can take his word seriously, not from afar but face to face with the people of the city. We can do unto others as we want them to do to us.

That would revolutionize our cities. It's not just another political plan. We serve our cities best by being faithful to God, by trusting that God himself will care for those in need. That he will solve our problems. This is not a call to do nothing. We must not ignore the city. Instead, God calls us to activism. He may solve the city's problems through us or through others. But meekly and humbly we admit it's not our plan that will succeed. We are merely those who are in the hands of God.

Joy in the City

If we will place ourselves in his hands, then our lament over the city and its problems—problems so serious, so permanent, so impervious to solution—will turn from a cry of pain to a song of joy.

> Sing, O Daughter of Zion;
> shout aloud, O Israel!
> Be glad and rejoice with all your heart,
> O Daughter of Jerusalem!
> The Lord has taken away your punishment,
> he has turned back your enemy.
> The Lord, the King of Israel, is with you;
> never again will you fear any harm.
> The Lord your God is with you,
> he is mighty to save.
> He will take great delight in you,
> he will quiet you with his love,
> he will rejoice over you with singing.
> "At that time I will deal with all who
> oppressed you;
> I will rescue the lame
> and gather those who have been
> scattered.
> I will give them praise and honor
> in every land where they were put to
> shame.
> At that time I will gather you;
> at that time I will bring you home.
> I will give you honor and praise
> among all the peoples of the earth
> when I restore your fortunes before your
> very eyes,"
> says the Lord.
> Zephaniah 3:14,15, 17,19-20

I know it sounds like a political speech, but here is the solution to the problem of our cities. We even have the candidate who can solve our problems—the King, the Lord in our midst. If we, individually, as churches, and as a community put the Lord first in our lives, if we place him in the middle of all that we do and all that we are, then it is the power of God that will change our cities. It is God who will take the lame, the outcast, and all those in need, and will lift them up and exalt them.

It is God who will make Jerusalem, or Nashville, or even L. A. his city.

True, cities don't look good in Scripture. Cain starts the first one. There's Sodom, Gomorrah, and Babylon. But in addition to the evil city, Babylon the Great, mentioned in Revelation, there is another city. When Jesus wants to reveal to John what it will be like to see God face to face and enjoy him forever, he shows him a city. Cities tend to corrupt. They are generally evil. But our God is so powerful he can take even a city and make it his.

The new Jerusalem comes down from heaven. It's like no city you've ever seen. It's a pure city, a holy city. Readied as a bride for her husband. And in that new Jerusalem, there will be no poverty, no injustice, no violence, no crime, no pain, no fear. The Lord God himself will wipe away every tear.

The beauty of that city is not its high walls of precious stones. It's not the beautiful park with the river of life. It's not streets of gold. The center of the city, the greatest thing about the city, is that it has no temple. Why? "Because the Lord God Almighty and the Lamb are its temple" (Revelation 21:22).

We live in cities that are great in many ways. Great and majestic, but also corrupt and full of pain, injustice, poverty, and crime. But even in the days of Zephaniah, God promises, "at that time I will bring you home."

What does God call us to do? He calls us to look forward to that great city we will someday enjoy. To wait for its coming. But he reminds us that as we wait for that new Jerusalem, our home, we also have a responsibility toward this city, the one in which we now live. We must be his faithful people, his remnant. Show his love to others. Proclaim to them, no matter how hopeless it seems, that the Lord is in the middle of our city. If we simply turn to him, then he will bless. He will heal. He will wipe away our tears and he will call us home.

Questions for Discussion

1. What do you think is the greatest problem facing your city? What is the solution?

2. Are people who live outside cities better than those in the city? Why is the Bible so negative about cities? What does the city do to people?

3. What are some recent stories you know about corrupt city officials? Can politicians solve the city's problem? What do they promise to get elected?

4. What are some recent stories you know about corrupt religious leaders in your city? What are religious leaders, including those in your church, doing to try to help the city?

5. How do we live as a righteous remnant in the city? What can we do to help others live that way?

Eight

How Can We Make the Church Grow?

Haggai 1:5-11

Is it a time for you yourselves
to be living in your paneled houses,
while this house remains a ruin?
Haggai 1:4

How can we make the church grow? An interesting question. But first we have to answer this one: "Do we really want the church to grow?" We might want it to grow for several reasons. It's exciting to be part of a growing church. We feel a sense of accomplishment and blessing when we see swelling numbers.

But for many, a growing church brings discomfort.

We look around and don't recognize many people. It's not the same old familiar faces. Things would not be the way they've always been; we'd have to make some changes. And change is always disorienting and painful for some.

Do we want the church to grow? At one level, we don't need the church, at least our own congregation, to grow for God to accomplish his purposes. We dare not make the mistake of thinking it's all up to us, that we must make the church grow for God's will to be done. In the Bible, God usually doesn't care about numbers. In the Gideon story, there are too many for God to accomplish his will (Judges 7). He has to cut the army down. David is punished for numbering his fighting men, because he was depending on his superior numbers to win battles instead of relying on the power of God (2 Samuel 24). God can do his will with many or few, great or small.

So why should we want the church to grow? Because we want all who will to come to God. Like God himself, we want no one to perish but all to repent (2 Peter 3:9). We want all to know the joy of salvation and the peace of being in Jesus. That's why we want the church to grow.

A Prophet of Growth

How can we make it grow? In the last several years a whole "science" of church growth has developed. There are hundreds of books with techniques to promote a growing church. This may all be a response to certain polls that show church attendance is down in America. Some of these techniques may help to grow the church, but where in Scripture would we find a plan for growing churches?

One place few have looked is in the Book of

Haggai. That's not surprising since Haggai had no church. What can an Old Testament book tell us about church growth? More than you might expect. Haggai is not concerned with the church but is involved in building (or actually re-building) God's temple.

We know the story. The Babylonians destroyed the temple when they carried Judah off to captivity (2 Kings 25:9). For almost seventy years the temple mound was a ruin. Under Ezra, Zerubbabel, and Nehemiah, those who had returned from exile faced the daunting task of rebuilding the temple. Haggai was God's cheerleader for that task.

But what does rebuilding the temple have to do with making the church grow? Christians do not worship in temples today. Church buildings are tools used to the glory of God. They are important places because we meet God there. We might even call them sanctuaries, but God does not inhabit them in the same way his glory filled the Jerusalem temple.

Instead, in the New Testament, God's glory fills not a building but a people. The church (the people, not the building) is God's temple, the place where he shows his glory. Paul often describes himself as a builder, as in this word to the Corinthians.

> By the grace God has given me, I laid a foundation as an expert builder, and someone else is building on it. But each one should be careful how he builds. For no one can lay any other foundation other than the one already laid, which is Jesus Christ.
>
> Don't you know that you yourselves are God's temple and that God's Spirit lives in you? If anyone destroys God's temple, God will destroy him; for God's temple is sacred, and you are that temple.
>
> 1 Corinthians 3:10-11, 16-17

The "you" here is plural in Greek. It's not just that each of us individually is a temple of God; it's that we are together being built into his temple.

So we go back to Haggai and view his struggles in motivating God's people to build the temple. By doing so, we can discover insights into the struggle we go through to build God's temple, the church.

To the Work

What does it take to build or rebuild a temple? A church? First of all, it takes people who want to build and are willing to work. At the beginning of Haggai's ministry, he faced a people who were not willing to work. God speaks to Haggai with words for those people.

> This is what the Lord Almighty says:
> "These people say, 'The time is not yet
> come for the Lord's house to be built.'"
> Haggai 1:2

The time is not yet come. Have you ever heard people at your church say, "Well, we hope the Lord will bless us with growth, maybe he will someday, but this is just not the right time to start a new program." Why would someone feel that way? Why did those in Haggai think that way? Because in their mind they had other, more pressing duties.

> Then the word of the Lord came through
> the prophet Haggai: "Is it a time for you
> yourselves to be living in your paneled
> houses while this house of mine
> remains a ruin?"
> Haggai 1:3-4

Why is it they were not rebuilding the house of the Lord? Because they were too busy improving and remodeling their own houses. They wanted "paneled houses." I'm not sure what is the contemporary equivalent of a "paneled house," but it sounds like much more than basic shelter. As I write these words, I feel somewhat hypocritical. We just paid to have our house repainted and the workmen are building us a new carport at the moment. Does God condemn home improvement? Perhaps—if we're more concerned about our own comfort and luxury than we are about the house of the Lord.

Might it be at times that the reason we do not work to make the church grow is that we have more pressing issues? Like what? Home improvement, a new car, dental work for the kids? Should we work overtime or get a second job? Everyone else has "paneled houses." Shouldn't we have them, too, even if it means work and worry and neglect of the house of God? Could God say to us, "You are too worried about how you live, and not concerned enough about me."

Work and Blessing

Not only do those in Haggai's day care too much about themselves, they also have not taken the big view.

> Now this is what the Lord Almighty says, "Give careful thought to your ways. You have planted much, but harvested little. You eat, but never have enough. You drink, but never have your fill. You put on clothes, but are not warm. You earn wages, only to put them in a purse with holes in it."
> Haggai 1:5-6

There is an irony about caring first about yourself and looking out for number one. If we do place ourselves ahead of God, then ultimately we are not really taking care of ourselves. So the Lord says, "While you're worried about your paneled houses, take an honest look at your financial condition." It's a picture many of us find uncomfortably familiar. We earn our wages and put them in a bag with holes. Where does the money go? Why is it that no matter how much we make there's never any left over at the end of the month? Why can't we get ahead financially?

Because we do not put God first.

> This is what the Lord Almighty says: "Give careful thought to your ways. Go up into the mountains and bring down timber and build the house, so that I might take pleasure in it and be honored," says the Lord. "You expected much, but see, it turned out to be little. What you brought home, I blew away. Why?" declares the Lord Almighty. "Because of my house which remains a ruin, while each of you is busy with his own house. Therefore, because of you the heavens have withheld their dew and the earth its crops. I called for a drought on the fields and the mountains, on grain, and the new wine, the oil, and whatever the ground produces, on men and cattle, and on the labor of your hands."
> Haggai 1:7-11

"You don't really care about my house," God says. "And that's why things are going so badly for you." That's certainly true: this is the Bible, after all. But this is one of those dangerous passages in the Bible, dangerous because it has been misunderstood. Not all financial suffering is the result of faithlessness toward God.

Instead this passage says what Jesus later restates in the Sermon on the Mount: "But seek first his kingdom and his righteousness, and all these things will be given to you as well" (Matthew 6:33). Like Haggai, Jesus is talking to those with financial worries. "Will we have enough to eat? What will we drink? How can we afford clothes?" Jesus says, "Don't worry about those things. Seek the kingdom first, and God will take care of you."

Where Haggai and maybe even Jesus have been more often misunderstood is by making their words the guarantee of a health and wealth gospel. "You give to God and he will reward you financially." Certainly, God might reward us that way, but it doesn't happen all the time. Sometimes you can give your whole heart and effort to the Lord and things will get worse, financially and otherwise. Worse in the short term, at least.

But the promise of Haggai and Jesus still is true. If we give our hearts wholly to God, to his kingdom, if we place his house, his church, above even our own houses, then God will bless us. It may be financially: he will take care of food, clothing, and shelter—the basic needs of life. More importantly, God will bless us in ways we cannot imagine.

What does it take to make the church grow? We have to want it to grow. And that means putting God first. It means putting the church first. I know it's not the church that saves, it's Christ. But we dare not separate Christ and the church. It is his body. We are God's temple.

If we gave a little more effort, more time, concern, and prayer about building up the church, then what would God do? He'd bless us. He'd work his will in ways we can't imagine. He would build his temple.

Work in Faith

The people in Haggai's day heard the promise that God would act, so they started to build the temple. However, after they began they faced disappointment.

> On the twenty-first day of the seventh month, the word of the Lord came through the prophet Haggai: "Speak to Zerubbabel son of Shealtiel, governor of Judah, to Joshua son of Jehozadek, the high priest, and to the remnant of the people. Ask them, 'Who of you is left who saw this house in its former glory? How does it look to you now? Does it not seem to you like nothing?'"
> Haggai 2:1-3

What does it take to grow God's church? It takes effort. But we must not fall into the trap of thinking that human effort is all it takes. We must not think that with a bit more effort or a new evangelism technique or a new worship model we can make the church what it should be.

Perhaps that's what happened in Haggai's day. They started rebuilding and those older folks who could remember the glory of the earlier temple became discouraged. "You call this a temple?" they asked. "This is nothing compared to the good old days."

Sometimes, we do grow discouraged when we compare our plans and accomplishments to what has gone before us. We think the church was in better shape twenty years ago or forty years ago. Perhaps it was. Or we compare ourselves to the first century church and we don't seem to stack up to their dedication and growth.

Perhaps the reason we get discouraged is because we put all the burden on ourselves. It's up to us to make this temple look good. The way this plays out in our day involves all those books and all those techniques of church growth. Of course, there's nothing wrong with plans to grow the church or techniques to help bring people into the church. The trouble comes when we trust too much in our plans and techniques.

Think of the methods we've used throughout the years. If you are my age or older you remember filmstrips, bus ministries, cottage meetings, friendship evangelism, seminars, worship workshops, and the list goes on. It's not that any of these were bad or wrong. The problem is that with each new technique there are some who think, "This is it. We've now found the key. We now know *the* way to make the church grow."

Haggai reminds us that when we have done all that we can do, the glory of the temple is not a matter of human effort. It's the glory of God. No plan, no technique can build the church without the power of God. Looking back and longing for "the good old days" cannot make the church better without the power and glory of God.

So what does it take to make the church grow? It takes people willing to work, but aware that all their efforts are, by themselves, futile. What we need to do is let God build his temple. Let God build his church.

He may do that through us. I pray he does. But we must remember it is God, not us, who is building.

Go back to Solomon and that first great temple in Jerusalem, the temple those in Haggai's day were longing for. When Solomon dedicates the temple, he acknowledges that no building can contain God (1 Kings 8:27). He does not live in a house made with human hands. God is greater than the temple. It is an important building not because of its size or its beauty or as a showplace for the greatest human craftsmen.

What makes the temple magnificent is that the Lord God places his glory, his presence there.

The True Beauty of the Temple

Later in Haggai, having said that the temple looks like nothing to some, God makes this promise:

> "But now be strong, O Zerubbabel," declares the Lord. "Be strong, O Joshua son of Jehozadak, the high priest. Be strong, all you people of the land," declares the Lord, "and work. For I am with you," declares the Lord Almighty. "This is what I covenanted with you when you came out of Egypt. And my Spirit remains among you. Do not fear." This is what the Lord Almighty says: "In a little while I will once more shake the heavens and the earth, the sea and the dry land. I will shake all nations, and the desired of all nations will come, and I will fill this house with glory," says the Lord Almighty. "The silver is mine and the gold is mine," declares the Lord Almighty. "The glory of this present house will be greater than the glory of the former house," says the Lord Almighty. "And in this place I will grant peace," declares the Lord Almighty.
> Haggai 2:4-9

God makes an amazing promise through Haggai. This ramshackle, makeshift building (nothing compared to Solomon's temple) will be greater than Solomon's. This will not be the result of human effort, although it takes human effort. God says "work," but it is God who is with them. It is God who will shake down all the nations. He will take what is his (and everything is his) and bring it into this temple. The later glory of that house will be greater than the former.

Again, what does that have to do with the church? Why doesn't the church grow like we want it to? Why doesn't the church grow like it should? Maybe because we're not giving the effort we should. We are more concerned about our own houses, comfort, and luxury.

But perhaps there's another reason, a deeper reason. Maybe we're not trusting God to be at work in his house. We don't see him there at work alongside us.

I am part of a small church. There are great things about small churches, or at least about ours. We know one another. We love one another. We share our hopes, our fears, and our failures. But as a small church we can sometimes think that we cannot accomplish much for God. The big churches are where the action is. They have more ministers than we have members. They have the growing, exciting programs for every age group. Eight softball teams. Three bowling leagues. A physical plant that looks like it should be producing automobiles. We look like nothing compared to them. Our church is not even as large as it was twenty years ago. What can we do?

The answer is: we can do as much as God can do. And that's a great deal. How can one accomplish more than the all-powerful God?

Haggai reminds this group of downtrodden, former exiles, "Don't look at the little you can do. Look at what God can do." He can take our poor efforts and make the greatest temple that has ever been. He not only can, he will.

Back to Paul and the Corinthians. Paul talks about his role as the builder of the Corinthian church. He mentions others who built on his foundation. Then he changes the metaphor to farming. "I planted the seed, Apollos watered it, but God made it grow" (1

Corinthians 3:6).

What does it take to grow the church? People who are willing to work, but also willing to trust. To trust the God who can take the smallest, most insignificant seed and make it a huge plant; to trust the Son of God who reminds us that the seed grows by itself. Yes, we plant and water and cultivate. But God alone gives growth.

This is not a call to apathy. We dare not say by our actions, "Okay, God, it's your church. Grow it without me." He can. He can do it all without us. But he loves us enough to call us to work with him.

God's call is also not a call to an unfocused activism. We work but we also wait for him to give the increase. We cannot bring in the kingdom through our own efforts.

He calls us to faithfulness, to work for the Lord. To let him build us, no matter how painful that may be. If we let him, we too will be beautiful with his glory.

Questions for Discussion.

1. What are reasons that some Christians give for not wanting their church to grow? Are these legitimate concerns?

2. What is God's temple today? What are the implications of being God's temple?

3. What are some ways in which we can make our "paneled houses" more important than God's house?

4. If we work for God, are we promised financial prosperity? What are we promised?

5. Can we grow the church without techniques and plans? Can we depend too much on our techniques

and plans? How can we be active in promoting church growth and still trust God to provide it?

Nine

What Should We Teach Our Children?

Joel 1:1-3

"Tell it to your children,
and let your children tell it to their children,
and their children to the next generation."
Joel 1:3

A child cries out in the middle of the night. His mother comes to his room, takes him in her arms, and says, "Hush now. It's all gonna be all right."

Did the mother just lie to her little boy?

Teach Your Children Well

We live in a strange age. An age where many family therapists, psychologists, and even many parents believe we should not impose our values on our children. Particularly in the areas of morality and religion, we are to let them make their own decisions.

This may take the form of the question, "Do you make you children go to church?" Some feel you should not make a child go to church no matter what his or her age, because it will turn the child against religion.

But the truth is, it is not good policy for Christians to raise their children without speaking of God. It's not only bad policy, but I'm not sure it can even be done. Can we really be neutral about faith in God?

Back to our first question. When that mother goes in, takes her little boy in her arms, and says, "It's all going to be all right," is she lying? Some would say, "Yes, she is." After all, she really can't guarantee that it is going to be all right. She doesn't know the tragedies that might be in store for her son.

But even if it is a lie, surely it's a forgivable one. It's the kind of thing we say to comfort our children. But what about those of us who have faith in God? When we take our children in our arms and say, "Don't cry; it will be all right," we mean it. We believe that ultimately it's all going to be all right. When we comfort our children this way we are doing what we have done many times before. We are telling them a story that goes like this. "Even though things are bad here and you are frightened and scared, it's all part of a larger story that has a happy ending. It will be all right. God will make it all right." We are not lying to our children but telling them a true story, the greatest story of all.

The Power of Story

What do we teach our children? How do we teach our children about God? There are many things we should teach. There are many ways we do teach. We teach by how we live. We teach them about the Bible. We teach them what they ought to do and what they shouldn't do. But the most effective, powerful, and biblical way to teach our children is by telling stories.

Didn't your parents tell you stories? Didn't you love to hear them? Don't we still delight in the pleasure of a good story? Stories tell truths that cannot be told in other ways. Bare facts don't have the power of stories.

My dad loved me growing up. That's a fact. But it has more impact when I tell it as a story. My mom passed away with cancer when I was twelve and my brother was five. Dad worked as an airline mechanic and had just been promoted to lead mechanic. However, in his new position he lacked seniority and so had to work the late afternoon and evening shift. Dad wanted and needed to be home with his boys. So he gave up his promotion and went back to being an ordinary mechanic so he could have seniority and work the day shift. He was never again promoted. By that act, Dad taught me more about love and work and the place of family than he ever taught me in words. The power is in the story of Dad's love.

We all have great stories, family stories, that tell us that we are loved, that tell us who we are.

The Story of Deliverance

Let's look at three great stories. Or perhaps one great story told three ways.

In Deuteronomy, the question, "What do we teach

our children?" is a live one. It had been forty years since the Exodus. A new generation had arisen who were not slaves in Egypt, who had not crossed the Red Sea, and who had not seen the fire of God on Sinai. How should that generation and future generations be taught?

> In the future, when your son asks you,
> "What is the meaning of the stipulations, decrees, and laws the Lord our God has commanded you?" tell him...
> Deuteronomy 6:20

Before we get to the answer, notice the question. The kids will ask, "Mom, Dad, why does God say, 'Do this' or 'Don't do that?'" It's a question about stipulations, decrees, and laws. The answer may seem obvious. When our children ask about God's laws, we should explain the purpose and meaning of the laws. But that's not the way God tells them to answer.

> ...tell him: "We were slaves of Pharaoh in Egypt, but the Lord brought us out of Egypt with a mighty hand. Before our eyes the Lord sent miraculous signs and wonders—great and terrible—upon Egypt and Pharaoh and his whole household. But he brought us out from there to bring us in and give us the land that he promised to our forefathers. The Lord commanded us to obey these decrees and to fear the Lord our God, so that we might always prosper and be kept alive, as is the case today. And if we are careful to obey all this law before the Lord our God, as he has commanded us, that will be our righteousness."
> Deuteronomy 6:21-25

The children say, "Why do we have all these rules, these decrees, these laws?" Moses says, when you get the question, you don't explain; you tell them a story. "We were slaves in Egypt, but God remembered us. Because we are his people he led us out of Egypt, destroying the Egyptians with plagues. God did not abandon us in the wilderness when we left Egypt, but he gave us these laws for our own good. If we keep his decrees, then we are right with God and he will bless us."

It's the same way today. We get the same questions from our kids. Why is it wrong to do a certain thing? Why do we do the same old things at church? What do those acts mean? Why does God give us so many rules? We answer with a story, this story of God's deliverance of his people from slavery. That's why we teach these stories in Sunday School.

But the stories are not just for children. They are not merely old stories that have little to do with us, although at first it may seem that way. Have you been a slave in Egypt? I've never even been to Egypt. Probably none of us have seen plagues of flies and hail and frogs. We've never gone marching in the wilderness with God.

Or have we? This is not just their story, the story of people long ago, this is our story. Notice how Moses says to tell the story. We don't say to our children, "Grandpa was down in Egypt." We say, "We were slaves in Egypt." Those who were to hear this story had never been to Egypt, yet they had been slaves there. It is their story. It's more than an account of how God led his people in the past; it's how he leads us now.

It's our story, our experience, our faith. God has led us from the slavery of sin into a land of promise. That's why we tell the story.

Earlier, Deuteronomy tells us when we should tell the story.

> Hear O Israel: The Lord our God, the Lord is one. Love the Lord your God with all your heart and with all your soul and with all your strength. These commandments I give you this day are to be upon your hearts. Impress them on your children. Talk about them when you sit at home and when you walk along the road, when you lie down and when you get up. Tie them as symbols on your hands and bind them on your foreheads. Write them on the doorframes of your houses and on your gates.
> Deuteronomy 6:4-8

When do we tell the story? We tell it all the time. When we get up. When we lie down. As we walk down the road. We tell it until the kids are tired of it. Then we tell it some more. This is what it means to be God's people. We are people with a story—a great story, a story of deliverance. We were slaves and God set us free.

The Story of Repentance

The story looks a bit different in the Book of Joel. Joel lived a long time after the Exodus. He also lived long ago, compared to our time. Joel also has a story to tell.

> Hear this, you elders;
> listen, all who live in the land.
> Has anything like this ever happened in
> your days
> or in the days of your forefathers?

> Tell it to your children,
> and let your children tell it to their children,
> and their children to the next generation.
> Joel 1:2-3

Joel says, "God is doing something in our day that has never been done before. We have that story to tell." So they tell it to their children, their grandchildren, and wait to tell it to generations yet unborn.

What's the story in Joel's day? It's a story that begins with bad news. Sounds familiar. What was the story in the time of Moses? It also began with bad news: we were slaves in Egypt. That's bad news. Joel's bad news sounds like this:

> What the locust swarm has left,
> the great locusts have eaten;
> what the great locusts have left,
> the young locusts have eaten;
> what the young locusts have left,
> other locusts have eaten.
> Joel 1:4

I don't know much about locusts. In Hebrew, there are three types of locusts mentioned in these verses. The bad news is clear: the locusts are coming to eat the crops. We will have no food. We'll starve. If this is the story Joel wants us to tell our children, it wouldn't comfort them, but might make them wake up crying. What's the point of telling a story of starvation? It's bad news first, just like slavery in Egypt. God is going to punish Israel. The locusts are going to come.

But the story doesn't end there. God sends this plague of locusts not to harm his children but to move them to repent.

> "Even now," declares the Lord,
> "return to me with all your heart,
> with fasting and weeping and mourning."
> Rend your heart and not your garments.
> Return to the Lord your God,
> for he is gracious and compassionate,
> slow to anger and abounding in love,
> and he relents from sending calamity.
> Then the Lord will be jealous for his land
> and take pity on his people.
> The Lord will reply to them:
> "I am sending you grain, new wine and oil,
> enough to satisfy you fully;
> never again will I make you
> an object of scorn to the nations."
> Joel 2:13, 18-19

Bad news—locusts are coming. Good news—it's for their own good. God sends this plague to turn them back to him. He wants them to tear their hearts, not just their clothes.

The end of the story in Joel is the best news of all. If we, like them, will turn back to God, then God will do in our day a marvelous thing. As in the days of Moses and Joel, he will lead us to the Promised Land and give us unimaginable blessings. In Joel the end of the story looks like this:

> In those days and at that time,
> when I restore the fortunes of Judah and
> Jerusalem…
> The Lord will roar from Zion and thunder
> from Jerusalem;
> the earth and the sky will tremble.
> But the Lord will be a refuge for his people,
> a stronghold for the people of Israel.
> "Then you will know that I, the Lord your
> God,
> dwell in Zion, my holy hill.
> Jerusalem will be holy; never again will
> foreigners invade her.

> Judah will be inhabited forever
> and Jerusalem through all generations.
> Their bloodguilt, which I have not
> pardoned, I will pardon."
> The Lord dwells in Zion!
> Joel 3:1, 16-17, 20-21

Joel begins with bad news—the locusts are coming. But it ends with a story that must be shared with our children and our children's children, a story of a gracious, forgiving God who wants us to return to him. And when we return he becomes our Fortress, our Provider, our Savior. He promises to be with his people forever.

Our Story

This is our story, not just Joel's or Israel's story.

We were slaves—slaves to sin. And God delivered us and led us forth with a mighty hand, the hand of his Son. He led us to a Promised Land, a New Jerusalem. Even after he brought us there, we turned our backs on God. So, like a loving father, he has disciplined us and punished us, all to get us to turn back to him. And if we do, he promises us that he will be our God and we will be his people. He will be our fortress and nothing will harm us.

It's the same story in Deuteronomy and Joel, the same story told two ways. Now for a third way.

This time the story is not passed down from parent to child but from one who knows the story to those who want to know. In Acts 10, Peter goes to the house of Cornelius, the gentile. Peter is reluctant to go, but God sends him a vision, so he goes. Cornelius is not a child, but as far as his knowledge of God goes, he is like a child in his understanding. With a child-like heart,

Cornelius wants to know more.

Where does Peter begin? Not with commandments, as we might expect him to do in talking with a gentile. No, he doesn't even begin with, "Here's what you need to do to be saved." He begins with a story. An old, old story, but a powerful one.

> You know the message God sent to the people of Israel, telling the good news of peace through Jesus Christ, who is Lord of all. You know what has happened throughout Judea, beginning in Galilee after the baptism that John preached—how God anointed Jesus of Nazareth with the Holy Spirit and power, and how he went around doing good and healing all who were under the power of the devil, because God was with him. We are witnesses of everything he did in the country of the Jews and in Jerusalem. They killed him by hanging him on a tree, but God raised him from the dead on the third day and caused him to be seen.
> Acts 10:36-40

Peter begins the story with bad news, just as Moses does: we were slaves in Egypt. Just as Joel begins: the locusts are coming. But Peter's news is worse. God sent his Son. Jesus the Messiah came and evil people put him to death.

But the bad news soon turns to good news. God raised him on the third day. The resurrected Jesus appeared to witnesses. Peter is one of those witnesses. And then the greatest news of all. "Everyone who believes in him receives forgiveness of sins through his name" (Acts 10:43).

Still, Our Story

Who are we as Christians? What does it mean to follow Jesus? Where do we get our identity? At least one answer is we are people with a story. Perhaps we can best describe ourselves as "tellers." Not the people who work in banks, but those who have a story and tell it. You can tell the story many ways: we were slaves and God led us to the Promised Land; we were faithless, so God punished us with locusts and famine. But he's a good and gracious God who takes away our punishment and becomes our fortress.

Or you can tell it Peter's way: "Let me tell you about Jesus." A man who went around doing good. More than a man, the promised Messiah, Son of God. He was put to death, but he rose again the third day and appeared to witnesses. If we follow this Jesus, we will have full salvation and forgiveness of sin.

We can tell it our own way. For me, it's a story passed down to me by loving parents. I can't remember a time I did not know it. Yet somewhere along the line I made it my story. I confessed my faith in Jesus and died with him in baptism. I was raised to new life.

My story. Your story, even though you may have come to faith in a slightly different way. What do we do with this story? We go and tell what God has done for us. We tell it to our children and to our children's children. We tell it to friends. We tell it to neighbors. We tell it to strangers. The story of deliverance, repentance, and forgiveness through Jesus Christ. We tell the truth when we say to ourselves, our children, and others, "It's going to be all right."

Questions for Discussion

1. What are some specific ways we can teach our children about God at home? When should we do this?

2. Does the story of the Bible always begin with bad news? If so, why is that?

3. How is our current situation like the Israelites in the time of Moses? How is it different?

4. Does God send us hard times today to get us to repent? Why or why not?

5. Why are we sometimes reluctant to tell the story of Jesus to others? How can we overcome that reluctance?

Ten

How Can I Reach My Neighbor?

Zechariah 8:20-23

In those days ten men from all languages
and nations will take firm hold of one Jew by the
hem of his robe and say, "Let us go with you,
because we have heard that God is with you."
Zechariah 8:23

Two older fellows were out fishing and reminiscing about their youth. "When I was a kid," one said, "we used to pull pranks on people by ringing their doorbells and running off before they came to the door." "That's funny," the other said. "We still do that at our church. We call it evangelism."

That may be what comes to our minds when we

think of evangelism. Knocking on stranger's doors, our knees shaking, hoping that no one comes to the door. At least that's my experience. As a shy (or, at least, private) person, I don't enjoy talking to strangers. To some that makes me unfit for evangelism, because we associate it with the friendly, never-met-a-stranger, talk-to-a-fencepost personality type.

Yet we all believe in evangelism and think we have a duty to tell the gospel to others. We know we should bring others to the Lord. We may fondly look back on a time when our church was one of the fastest-growing groups around. Some of us remember a time when we could assume our neighbors respected the Bible. If we could show them the Bible said something, then that settled it. Thirty years ago, much of what we called evangelism was more like Priscilla and Aquila teaching Apollos and "explaining the way of God more adequately" (Acts 18:26).

Times have changed. If it was difficult to evangelize then, it seems much harder today. We cannot take it for granted that our neighbors know the Bible. We can't assume they respect the Bible. So here we are without the personality type some associate with evangelism and in a country less and less Christian (if it ever truly was). We wonder where to begin in telling the good news. We ask, "How can I reach my neighbor?"

Easy Evangelism?

In my youth, evangelism sermons usually came from the Book of Acts, the great account of the growth of the early church. In Acts, evangelism seems awfully easy. You get up to speak and there are thousands of people there who want to hear what you say. You know they're interested because three thousand of them repent and are baptized.

It even happens with strangers. The Spirit tells you to go to a certain road. You go, and a stranger passes by reading from Isaiah 53, that great chapter on the suffering of the Messiah. You ask him if he understands what he is reading. He says, "No, come help me." So you preach Jesus to him and he is baptized. I think I could do that type of evangelism.

Or you see a vision and as soon as it ends there are strangers at the door asking you to come preach to a man and his family. I've never had anyone knock on my door and ask me to preach. But Peter goes and a man named Cornelius greets him at the door and says, "I've invited all my friends and family. We want to hear what you have to say."

Has that been your experience with evangelism? Even when we look at New Testament examples of evangelism, they don't fit our encounters with unbelievers. Those examples make it seem too easy.

So what do we do? Do we simply give up on efforts to evangelize? Do we say we don't have the right personality? Do we long for the good old days when people were more interested in the Bible and our churches were more full?

Old Testament Evangelism

To answer those questions let's turn to an Old Testament example of evangelism. We usually think of evangelism as a purely New Testament concept. After all, the gospel is about Jesus. But even under the old covenant, God intended Israel to be a blessing to all the nations. Through Abraham, God promised to bless all peoples (Genesis 12:3).

So we turn back to a time when Israel was not the blessing she should have been, the time of exile. It was a time when it was difficult to be an evangelist in Judah, for God's people were a small, powerless group, struggling to rebuild the temple and the city of Jerusalem. God's people were trying to be a blessing to others, but it wasn't that easy. They'd failed before. They'd known exile. They looked back to the good old days of David and Solomon, days when Israel was respected. They longed for the time when it was easier to be a blessing.

Which brings us to the Book of Zechariah, a prophet who writes after the exile. He writes to a discouraged Judah, to a people who know what it's like not to be blessed by God. Their ancestors had turned their backs on God and suffered his punishment. Now this generation needs to learn what it means to have God's blessing and how to be a blessing to others.

The name Zechariah means "the Lord remembers." In that name we find a clue as to how these returned exiles are to be a blessing to their neighbors. We also find the key to how we are to tell good news to our neighbors. Zechariah tells Judah there will come a time when evangelism is easy.

> And many peoples and powerful nations
> will come to Jerusalem to seek the Lord Almighty and to entreat him.
> This is what the Lord Almighty says: "In those days ten men from all languages and nations will take firm hold of one Jew by the hem of his robe and say, 'Let us go with you, because we have heard that God is with you.'"
> Zechariah 8:22-23

That's the kind of evangelism I want. I want people to pass me on the street, grab me by my coat and say, "Can we please go to church with you?" I'd like it even better if those people were from every nation and said, with all kinds of languages and accents, "We want to come and be with you." That's what God says will happen. All nationalities will hold to the Jews and say, "We've heard God is with you. Let us come and be with you."

A People with God among Us

What is it in Zechariah's day that draws all nationalities to God and his people? Earlier in Zechariah, there is a long string of promises from God. It was those promises that drew strangers to the Jews and to their God.

What are those promises? The first is that God will live with his people.

> Again the word of the Lord Almighty came to me. This is what the Lord Almighty says: "I am very jealous for Zion; I am burning with jealousy for her."
> This is what the Lord says: "I will return to Zion and dwell in Jerusalem. Then Jerusalem will be called the City of Truth, and the mountain of the Lord Almighty will be called the Holy Mountain."
> Zechariah 8:1-3

A People Who Care for Old and Young

What was it long ago that would make Gentiles, pagans, and strangers to God grab a Jew and say, "Tell me about your God"? It was that God lived in their city, in Zion or Jerusalem. But how could those strangers see that God was in the middle of his people?

They saw it in the way the Jews treated one another.

> This is what the Lord Almighty says: "Once again men and women of ripe old age will sit in the streets of Jerusalem, each with cane in hand because of his age. The city streets will be filled with boys and girls playing there."
> Zechariah 8:4-5

You can tell that God lives with a people by the way they treat those who are older. Can they sit safely by the side of the road? Do we give respect to them as fountains of wisdom? Perhaps one reason we are ineffective at evangelism today is the lack of honor we show the elderly. In Judah, they were not warehoused in retirement homes (out of sight and out of mind) but proudly displayed in the city streets.

The way we treat children also reflects our relationship to God. When our neighborhoods and cities are safe enough for children to play in, then we have shown genuine concern for them. When children are neglected and abused, God is not living in our midst.

How can we evangelize? Perhaps it has more to do with keeping the streets safe than in knocking on doors. The way we treat those at the margins of society—the old and the young—displays our reverence or contempt for God. When people are too young or to old to be "useful" to a society, they need the particular help of God and his people. Our society's approval of killing the unborn and assisting in the suicides of the elderly shows contempt for God. The church must oppose such practices by both word and deed. We must do more than give lip service to the family while we go about our selfish, consumerist lives.

Only by serving the old and the young, the poor and the powerless, can we draw people to our God.

A People Who Trust the God Who Gathers

How else will strangers be drawn to God? When they see God's people trust in the One who can do the impossible.

> This is what the Lord Almighty says: "It may seem marvelous to the remnant of this people at that time, but will it seem marvelous to me?" declares the Lord Almighty.
> This is what the Lord Almighty says: "I will save my people from the countries of the east and the west. I will bring them back to live in Jerusalem; they will be my people, and I will be faithful and righteous to them as their God."
> Zechariah 8:6-8

Others are drawn when they see the trust God's people place in him. Judah was to trust that God could do what seemed too marvelous, even impossible to them. God could and would gather his people back to the land of promise. We also must trust God to protect his people and to gather others together with them. Perhaps we find evangelism hard because it is based on human ability and technique instead of on the power of God. Nothing is too great or marvelous for him.

A People of Prosperity

The prosperity of God's people can also draw others to him.

> But now I will not deal with the remnant of
> this people as I did in the past,"
> declares the Lord Almighty.
> "The seed will grow well, the vine will yield
> its fruit, the ground will produce its
> crops, and the heavens will drop their
> dew. I will give all these things as an
> inheritance to the remnant of this
> people. As you have been an object of
> cursing among the nations, O Judah
> and Israel, so will I save you, and you
> will be a blessing. Do not be afraid, but
> let your hands be strong."
> Zechariah 8:11-13

It is a truth of Scripture that God causes his people to prosper. Israel is not only promised a land of milk and honey, but also promised that God will continue to bless them if they remain faithful. However, if they forget the Lord, the rains won't come, the crops will die, and the other nations will conquer them. Israel made the wrong choice. They forgot their God and he allowed them to be exiled. Now, in Zechariah, he takes the curse away and promises them new prosperity.

But as we have seen in the other Minor Prophets, the truth that God causes his people to prosper is easily misunderstood. The size of one's bank account is not equivalent to the size of God's approval and blessing. Zechariah begins here not with what comes from the vine or crops from the ground but with the blessing of peace. In Hebrew, they are literally promised they will sow their seed in peace.

How can people tell if God is with us? When they see in us the peace that passes understanding. When they know we trust God for our daily bread.

A People of Honesty and Justice

They also see it in the way we treat others. Some who claim to be God's people have a deserved reputation of praising him loudly on Sunday and taking advantage of others the rest of the week. Instead, God's people are to be honest and just toward all. That will draw outsiders to God.

> These are the things you are to do: Speak the truth to each other, and render true and sound judgment in your courts; do not plot evil against your neighbor, and do not love to swear falsely. "I hate all this," declares the Lord.
> Zechariah 8:16-17

What would make a foreigner who despises Jews—particularly in their time of weakness—turn to the God of the Jews? When he sees these are people who treat others the way he wants to be treated. They speak the truth. They do no evil to their neighbors. They are just and fair, particularly to those who are weak. If we are honest and fair, others will notice.

A People of Praise

One more thing makes strangers cling to the people of God. They see and hear us praising God with joy and gladness.

> Again the word of the Lord Almighty came to me. This is what the Lord Almighty says: "The fasts of the fourth, fifth, seventh, and tenth months will become joyful and glad occasions and happy festivals for Judah. Therefore, love truth and peace."
> Zechariah 8:18-19

I know few Christians who fast. Perhaps they do and hide it well. But for most of us, fasting does not sound like a time of joy but a time of trial. But even fasting is a celebration if God is with us. One purpose of fasting is to focus our lives on God. And with God comes joy.

So, How Do We Reach Our Neighbors?

God says to Judah, "If you let me live among you, here's what will happen. Old people will sit in the gates. Your kids will run and play safely in the streets. I will do the impossible and gather my people together. I'll give you prosperity. You will treat one another with justice and honesty. There will be seasons of joy, gladness, and worship."

But how in the world is this relevant to us? Isn't it a great stretch to go from Zechariah to evangelism? Can we use this passage to answer the question, "How do I reach my neighbor?" We are grasping for an answer to that question. The old methods don't work. I don't despise those methods. My parents probably would not have become Christians without filmstrips and cottage meetings (later known as home Bible studies). But times have changed. We now try friendship evangelism or seeker worship. Or we give up and stop trying to evangelize.

Perhaps we have lost sight of what is central about evangelism, or reaching our neighbors *for God*. What is central is that it is for God. It is God who remembers Judah. Yes, in one sense, they must remember him, but the initiative is with God himself. Zechariah's name means, "The Lord remembers." He remembers his people. He brought them back to Jerusalem. He lives among them. That's why ten foreigners will grab one Jew and say, "Let us go with you." Because they have heard the Lord is with them (Zechariah 8:23).

We move to the Gospel of Luke and find it begins with another Zechariah. God remembers again. We have a greater story than the Jews had. God has done more for us than restore our fortunes and bring us from exile. He has freed us from sin. Zechariah fathers John the Baptist. John prepares the way for Jesus. It is in Jesus that God has remembered his people—remembered, forgiven, redeemed, and blessed. He lives among us. He lives in us, through his Son.

We remember it's God's world, not ours, God's kingdom, not ours. It is God's church, not ours. It is Christ's church. And if people are going to come to Christ's church, Christ must call them. How does Christ call? In many ways, some mysterious to us, He opens their hearts to hear the message (Acts 16:14).

He can even use us to open their hearts. He will cause our neighbors—real people, people we know—to look at us and say, "There's something different about you. God is somehow with you in a way I can't quite fathom or understand. Let me go with you. Tell me more."

What will draw our neighbors? When they see God among us. How do they see it? The same way the strangers saw it among the Jews. We care for the old and young. We are fair toward all. We praise God every moment of every day. We trust God for blessing and prosperity.

Will there come a time when every pew in our churches is full, a time when evangelism is easy? I don't know. I have no plan that can suddenly make it happen. But I do know we serve a God who can do marvelous things. If he wills it, every pew will be full.

People will grab us and ask to come. God is at work; what we must do is work with him. The key to evangelism is to trust the God who can do the impossible: to trust him with our lives. To trust him so much that we will love those around us.

That's how we reach them.

Questions for Discussion

1. Are we less evangelistic now than we used to be? If so, why?

2. What comes to mind when you hear the word, "evangelism"? Do we need to change our views on what constitutes evangelism?

3. How does your church treat the elderly? How does it treat children? Is your church involved in making the community better for the old and the young?

4. How can genuine, heart-felt praise draw the outsider to Christ? Is there a place for evangelism in worship?

5. Is God really among us? How do we show he is? How do we sometimes fail to show it?

Eleven

How Much Should I Give?

Malachi 3:7-12

Will a man rob God? Yet you rob me.
But you ask, "How do we rob you?"
In tithes and offerings.
Malachi 3:8

After reading the title of this chapter, you may be tempted to skip it. We tend to get upset about lessons on giving. Perhaps we feel that way for good reason. Some of us grew up in churches where we heard "the sermon on the amount" more than the Sermon on the Mount. Perhaps we are embarrassed by lessons on giving because they make the church seem money-grubbing, like some televangelists who always ask for money. Discussing giving and money appears less spiritual than other topics we could focus on. By definition, money is material. Thus mentioning money seems materialistic.

We particularly don't like to hear about tithing. A tithe is ten percent of our income, and any mention of taking 10% off the top sounds like taxes and government withholding (although we would be ecstatic if the government only took 10%). Is the church like the government, always wanting more of our money? Shouldn't church be more spiritual than that?

Money and Hearts

So why talk about giving? There's an old story from the time churches typically baptized in rivers. It was also before the days that baptismal garments became popular. A man came to be baptized. He and the minister waded into the river in their daily clothes. When they were almost hip deep, the man said, "Wait a minute, preacher, I forgot to take out my wallet." "Don't worry about it," the preacher replied, "we need to baptize that, too."

Whether or not we literally had it done, our wallets were baptized with us. Or at least they should have been. There is a close connection between our pocketbooks and our hearts. "For where your treasure is, there your heart will be also," said Jesus (Matthew 7:21). Money—what we do with it, how we earn it, how we spend it, and how often we think about it all say quite a bit about who we are deep down inside. How we handle money shows the extent of our spirituality.

This principle is found throughout the Bible. The amount we give back to God reflects our whole relationship with him. That's why the last book of the Old Testament, Malachi, calls Israel back to repentance. Or better, God calls his people to turn back to him. And turning involves their money.

> I the Lord do not change. So you, O
> descendants of Jacob, are not
> destroyed. Ever since the time of your
> forefathers you have turned away from
> my decrees and have not kept them.
> Return to me, and I will return to you,"
> says the Lord Almighty.
> But you ask, "How are we to return?"
> Will a man rob God? Yet you rob me.
> But you ask, "How do we rob you?"
> In tithes and offerings. You are under a
> curse—the whole nation of you—
> because you are robbing me."
> Malachi 3:6-9

God calls his people to return to him. What keeps them from returning? They are robbing God. That's strange language. How can anyone rob God? Can we take something away from God so that he doesn't have it anymore? Doesn't everything belong to God? How can we give him something he doesn't already have? And if we cannot really give him anything, we certainly cannot take anything away from him.

Do we really think when we write that check or reach into our pocket for the Sunday contribution that we are giving God something he didn't have before? Wasn't it God's money when it was in our bank account? Doesn't everything belong to God? The Psalmist says, "The cattle on a thousand hills are his" (Psalm 50:10). Today that would translate into, "The holdings of a thousand mutual funds." Everything belongs to God.

Not Part but All

What does God mean in Malachi when he asks, "Will a man rob God?" He immediately turns to tithes and offerings. We know what the tithe was—ten percent of their crops. Does God want ten percent of our gross salary? "No," we think, "that was the Old Testament." So we breathe a sigh of relief. But do we really think Jesus calls us to a lower standard than God had for his people in Old Testament times? Doesn't he call us to a higher righteousness? Shouldn't we give at least ten percent, or at least eleven, since we are called upon to do more than they did?

But what does it mean to tithe? Why should we tithe? First of all, the tithe is a way we recognize God as God. By tithing we are proclaiming that we owe all that we have and all that we are to God. It is a way of saying, "You are God and we are not."

God asks, "Will a man rob God?" to show us how ridiculous it is to think that anything belongs to us. When we withhold our tithe we say in effect to God, "This is mine, not yours." We say, "I am in control of my life, not you." We are even saying that we are gods, we are ultimately sovereign over our lives, which means God is not our God. To withhold the tithe is a selfish refusal to admit that we owe God everything.

This means we don't give our money because God needs it. The church really doesn't need our money. If that's true, then why have we been giving all these years? But it is true. The church is God's and he owns everything, all the riches of the universe. So why give? Because it is one way we recognize that everything belongs to God. When we give a tithe, a part of what we have, it represents everything we have and everything we are. We give it all to God.

We sometimes sing the hymn by Francis Havergal,

"Take my silver and my gold, not a mite would I withhold." Do we mean those words? We may not have much literal silver and gold. But not withholding a mite, that smallest biblical coin, means we are giving everything to God.

The mite language reminds us of that great story where Jesus and the disciples are watching people place various amounts in the contribution. Some placed generous amounts, large amounts. The disciples are impressed with those donors. But Jesus points to a woman who puts in two small coins, worth less than a penny. We probably would smile at someone who put pennies in the contribution or made change for a dollar. But Jesus says the woman gave more than all the rest (Luke 21:4).

How do we count the contribution? In some churches we still display the total on a board up front from week to week. That's our count, not God's. How does Jesus count the contribution? He says this widow gave the most because she gave all she had. That's all God wants. He wants everything. The part we put in the collection tray, the part we have in houses, clothes and cars, the part we have in our bank accounts and investments, it all belongs to God.

By tithing we confess that we own nothing. God has entrusted us with certain things for a while. But that's all we are, just money managers for God. If we refuse to give to God, we are saying, "Father, there is part of me that does not belong to you." We are robbing God, not of money, but of glory. We refuse to recognize who he is. We rob him of ourselves. And we are the ones who are impoverished.

Should we give a tenth? No, we should give it all, if we are God's people.

A Sign of Repentance

Tithing is also a sign of repentance. God says to his people, "Return to me." They ask, "How can we return?" We expect God to answer (at least in the New Testament), "Repent and be baptized." In the Old Testament, we expect him to say, "Put aside your foreign gods and worship only me." But instead God answers, "Here is how you return to me. Give me your tithes and offerings."

There is something about giving that is a sign of repentance, an admission that we have not been what we should have been. It is a sign that we want to come back to God.

Do not misunderstand. We cannot give our way back into good graces with God. He cannot be bribed, since everything is already his. This is not a call to make a fortune cheating others and then to give away millions to be "Citizen of the Year." It is a reminder that where our treasure is, our hearts are. What we do with our money is a sign of how seriously we take our relationship to God. Do we really want to follow God? Do we want to turn back to him? Do we want a closer walk with God?

One sign of repentance is how much we give. Do we give generously? Have we given God our money, our time, our efforts, not to buy his favor but to show our love? Paul praises the Macedonians who gave out of their poverty (2 Corinthians 8:1-5). Again, God does not count the amount we give, but he cares about the amount. Why? Because it reflects our heart. The Macedonians gave generously of their money. Why? Because "they gave themselves first to the Lord" (2 Corinthians 8:5).

It's not that God wants our money. He wants us. All of us. That means our money, too. The amount we give shows if we truly want relationship with God or if we are just playing at Christianity.

Remember the story in the Gospels about the perfect prospect who came to Jesus? He knows his Bible. He asks a good question, "What must I do to be saved?" He keeps God's commandments. He sounds like the best Christian we can imagine. He only lacks one thing. Jesus says, "Sell everything you have and give to the poor" (Luke 18:22). The man can't or won't. He goes away sad.

We read that story with a sigh of relief. We're glad Jesus doesn't demand that we sell everything and give it away. But doesn't he? Isn't Jesus giving this rich young man a test of repentance? "You say you want eternal life. How much do you want it? Are you willing to sell everything to get it?" Jesus asks us the same questions. Are we willing to sell everything we have—car, house, mutual funds, and retirement accounts—in order to follow Jesus?

Does Jesus require we sell it all? Perhaps. If it all gets in the way of repentance. He does require that we realize it is all his anyway. If we are not using our cars and houses and money to help the poor and serve God, we haven't truly turned to God. God calls us to return to him. "Come back," he says, "and bring all your stuff, too." If we give until it hurts, then we will rely on God, not on our money. The tithe shows repentance.

Give to Receive

God tells his people that if we just open up our tight fists and give, it will allow him to bless us more.

> "Bring the whole tithe into the storehouse,
> that there may be food in my house.
> Test me in this," says the Lord

> Almighty, "and see if I will not throw open the floodgates of heaven and pour out so much blessing that you will not have room enough for it. I will prevent pests from devouring your crops, and the vines in your fields will not cast their fruit," says the Lord Almighty. "Then all the nations will call you blessed, for yours will be a delightful land," says the Lord Almighty.
> Malachi 3:10-12

It's a cliché with some truth: you cannot outgive God. This is not an invitation to greed, but a call to trust. Ironically, if we hold on to our offerings out of fear we won't have enough, then we may not have enough. It is God who gives us daily bread, who makes the crops grow, and who keeps the pests away. Or, in our terms, God who gives a raise, a bonus, a larger bank account.

Again, this is no ironclad promise of financial success. It is a promise of God's care. As Jesus says, "Give, and it will be given to you. A good measure, pressed down, shaken together and running over, will be poured into your lap. For with the measure you use, it will be measured to you" (Luke 6:38). Or as Peter, who says he has left all to follow Jesus, is told,

> "I tell you the truth," Jesus replied, "no one who has left home or brothers or sisters or mother or father or children or fields for me and the gospel will fail to receive a hundred times as much in this present age (homes, brothers, sisters, mothers, children and fields—and with them, persecutions) and in the age to come, eternal life. But many who are first will be last, and the last first."
> Mark 10:29-31

The last phrase helps us understand the promise made in Malachi and by Jesus. This is not the greatest investment scheme of all time. Take what you gave last Sunday, multiply by a hundred, and expect the check this week. What is promised here is not instant financial success. We may still be last as far as the world is concerned and be first with God.

But we should not ignore the financial aspect of this promise. If we give generously to show our reliance on God, then we can rest assured that we can safely rely on him. He will give us what we need. He will give us more than we need so we can share with others.

Hasn't God kept this promise to us? A personal confession: I make more money than I need. What about you? Have you missed any meals lately because you couldn't afford food? Are you in danger of living on the street? Don't you have a little bit left over at the end of the month? If not, wouldn't you if you gave up all those things you don't really need? Hasn't God blessed us?

If not, perhaps it's because we don't give enough. We don't give enough to show we trust God. Perhaps we don't have enough because we are not grateful for what he has already given. Perhaps we don't have enough because we are never satisfied to have God alone.

But we're talking about much more than crops and bank accounts. If we open our hearts to be generous to others, if we freely give to God what is his, then he will give us more than money can buy: peace of mind; assurance that he will care for us; relationship with the Almighty. Hasn't he given us more than money can buy? He's given his Son. If God did not withhold his only Son from us, won't he also give us all things with Jesus (Romans 8:32)?

God says, "If you let me, I'll give you more than

you can imagine." That promise is still there. But if we don't receive what God has already given us with gratitude and generosity, how can he give more? Giving shows the size of our hearts. If we will not give, our hearts are too small to receive the outpouring of God's blessings.

Still, we are afraid to give sacrificially—afraid we won't have enough for our families. It's a fear that shows distrust of God. It's an irrational fear, because it goes against our own experience. As the Psalmist says,

> I was young and now I am old, yet I have
> never seen the righteous forsaken or
> their children begging bread.
> They are always generous and lend freely;
> their children will be blessed.
> Psalm 37:25-26

Some of us have been through hard times. But no matter how bad things have gotten, we can agree with the Psalmist: God has not abandoned his people. Those who are generous have never starved or begged. God is the greatest Giver. He will care for us and our children. Some of us may hesitate to give because we worry for our children. "If it were just me, I'd give more. But don't ask me to deprive my children." But we should not fear for their welfare because they are God's children, too. We care for them best by giving to others so God will give to them. We help them best by teaching them to rely on God alone.

So, How Much?

How much should we give? Perhaps our church leaders should sit down with every individual, couple, and family and tell them how much to give. Such a thought horrifies us. How dare they invade our privacy! But there is a connection with how much we give and our spiritual health. Shouldn't church leaders be concerned about our spiritual lives? Or do we think that money is completely divorced from spirituality?

Why do we hate sermons on giving? Perhaps for good reasons, perhaps for bad reasons. We think, "Yes, I want to be spiritual and closer to God, but what I do with my money is nobody's business." Or we at least think part of our money is ours.

How much should we give? That's between us and God, which makes it a serious question. Your church leaders probably don't know how much you make or how much you give. But God does.

How much should we give? For most of us the answer is "more." Even if we are giving generously, let's give more. Why? Does the church need your money? No. Does God need your money? No. We need to give more to constantly remind ourselves that God already has it all. We dare not rob God. He will care for us; our money won't. We need to give more to remind us that we come before God as penitent sinners. We give more as a sign of how much we want to be close to God.

Finally, it may sound strange, but we give more to God because we want more. Not more money, but more blessing: to know God more, to know Jesus and the power of his resurrection.

All God asks for is everything. All God gives is more than we can imagine.

Questions for Discussion

1. Do you react negatively to "giving sermons?" Why or why not? Should churches even have such lessons? Does the church talk too much about money?

2. Does money seem "unspiritual" to you? How does

our handling of money reflect what is really important to us? What does Jesus mean by "where your treasure is, there your heart will be?"

3. What keeps us from giving sacrificially?

4. Is it right to ask our children to suffer because of our generosity? Have you seen families suffer this way?

5. How does giving show repentance? What does it mean to "rob God?"

Twelve

What Does God Want From Us?

Micah 6:8

And what does the Lord require of you?
To act justly and to love mercy and to walk
humbly with your God.
Micah 6:8

I teach Bible at Lipscomb University in Nashville. At the beginning of every course I teach, I hand out a sheet with information important to me: the purpose of the course, what I hope to accomplish, how this study should change the lives of my students. The part that most interests students is the course requirements.

If you remember being a student, that's not surprising. They want to know if there will be tests, term papers, or other types of assignments. I do find it a bit disappointing that they care about requirements more than learning. For some students the concern about requirements is a way of asking, "What's the least amount I have to do to get an "A" (or a "B" or a "C")?"

Having said all that, asking about requirements makes a great deal of sense. When I came to teach at Lipscomb, what did I ask? "What does this job require?" I assume you asked the same at your last job interview. We'd be foolish not to ask. It's true of any assignment we are given. The boss says, "I'd like for you to be the chairperson of our United Way campaign this year." Wouldn't you ask, "What does that entail?"

What about church? Should we ask about requirements before we join? What about our whole relationship with God? Should we ask what he requires? It doesn't sound "religious" to ask such a question. But don't we all sometimes ask, "What does God want from me?"

Burdensome Requirements?

That question is asked and answered in the Book of Micah. It's in an interesting context. God has a dispute with his people. It's pictured as a legal case with God as the plaintiff and his people as the defendant. Who can judge such a case? God calls upon the mountains to judge.

> Listen to what the Lord says:
> "Stand up, plead your case before the
> mountains;
> let the hills hear what you have to say.
> Hear, O mountains, the Lord's accusation;
> listen, you everlasting foundations of the
> earth.
> For the Lord has a case against his people;
> he is lodging a charge against Israel."
> Micah 6:1-2

What does God have against his people? How have they wronged him? By accusing him of wronging them. God says he has done nothing but good to them.

> My people, what have I done to you?
> How have I burdened you? Answer me.
> I brought you up out of Egypt
> and redeemed you from the land of slavery.
> I sent Moses to lead you, also Aaron and Miriam.
> My people, remember what Balak king of Moab counseled
> and what Balaam son of Beor answered.
> Remember your journey from Shittim to Gilgal,
> that you may know the righteous acts of the Lord.
> Micah 6:3-5

God is suing his own people for lack of support. He says, "Why don't you turn back to me? Why don't you believe in me? Why don't you support me? Is it because of what I have done? How have I burdened you?" That's what God asks.

Do we ever think of our relationship with God as a burden? Isn't it a pain to get up on Sunday and come to church when we could sleep in and find better things to do? Writing the check for the contribution—isn't that a burden? Perhaps it's a burden in our personal relationships. There's that person at work who is out to get you. You have a marvelous chance to get them first. You didn't start this argument, but you have a chance to win it. But you say, "No. I can't do it. I have to treat them the way I want to be treated. The golden rule and all that." Isn't it a burden to be good?

We once knew a little boy not famous for his good behavior. When his mother would correct him, he'd always reply, "Aw, Mama. I'm tired of being good."

Don't we all sometimes feel that way? If we were honest, wouldn't we all sometimes say to Jesus, "Can't you just let up on me for a while?" It's not easy being good. Doesn't God sometimes ask too much? Aren't his requirements too tough?

Blessing, Not Burden

That's what the people in Micah's day thought. So God asks, "How? How have I burdened you? Did I burden you by saving you from Egypt? By freeing you from your enemies? Are my blessings a burden?" God did not come to burden them, but to free them. Our God has always been a God of freedom, not a God of burdensome details and rules.

Therefore their story is our story. If we are ever tempted to complain about the burdens God has given us, we must remember his yoke is easy and his burden is light. We were slaves to sin. God sent his only Son to take that burden away. We face enemies of all kinds: personal enemies—those people at work who are out to get us; those who make themselves our enemies because we are Christians; and the greatest enemy of all, Satan, that roaring lion who threatens to devour us. But God protects and sets us free from our enemies, whoever they might be.

What has God done for us? He has made us his children. He sets us free. He cares for us. Are those burdens? No, they are nothing but blessings. But still the question comes: What does God want from us? What are his requirements?

From our look at Malachi, we might think God just wants a little more money from us. Or a little more time and effort. That's what Judah thought in the time of Micah.

> With what shall I come before the Lord
> and bow down before the exalted God?
> Shall I come before him with burnt
> offerings,
> with calves a year old?
> Will the Lord be pleased with thousands of
> rams,
> with ten thousand rivers of oil?
> Shall I offer my firstborn for my
> transgression,
> the fruit of my body for the sin of my soul?
> Micah 6:6-7

Look at what God has given us. What does he want from us? How can we repay him? Let's give him more. Fat rams and oil. Checks and cash. Is that what God requires, that we give him a bit more?

Or does he require more than that? He gave his Son for us. Does he want our firstborn in return? Wouldn't God be within his rights to demand our firstborn child? But we know that he is not that kind of God. There were pagan gods who demanded child sacrifice, but surely not our God.

But if you read the Old Testament you find that is precisely what God required from his people. He tells Abraham to sacrifice Isaac (Genesis 22). He destroys the firstborn children of Egypt and tells Israel to offer their firstborn to him. Then, out of mercy, he allows them to redeem their firstborn with an animal sacrifice (Exodus 13:11-16). God did not demand they literally sacrifice their firstborn, but that is what they owed him.

Would we give the life of our firstborn to God? Wouldn't we instead give our own lives, give everything we had to save our child? But if we gave it all to God—our money, our lives, and our children—would it be enough to pay him back for all he has done for us? No. We can't give God enough. He gave his only child for us.

Do Justice

What does God want? What do we owe God? What does God require? Everything. And everything is not enough.

But here is what God will accept.

> He has showed you, O man, what is good.
> And what does the Lord require of you?
> To act justly and to love mercy and to walk
> humbly with your God.
> Micah 6:8

God's requirements make up a short list. Not hundreds of commands. Not even Ten Commandments. Just three. A list of requirements that may seem easy at first blush. Act justly, love mercy, and walk humbly. But if we look closely at these three requirements, they show that it's not what God wants that is essential. It's who God wants. He wants us to be his people. He wants us to have his character.

He wants us to act justly, to treat people fairly. The same thing we all were taught as kids. Play fair. Treat people right. Don't hit. Don't take what isn't yours.

As we get older, it becomes more difficult to know how to be fair to others. It means, when given the chance to take advantage of others, we never do. As Jesus put it, we treat others the way we want them to treat us. But it means more than that. The translation here, "act justly," is more accurately, "do justice." We are to bring in justice, to make our communities more just. This is more difficult than personally treating people fairly.

It's not enough to say, "I never personally cheated anyone." We must also look at those who have been treated unjustly by our society. We must work to create structures that make our society a bit more just. To speak up for those who are downtrodden and not allowed to speak for themselves. To put our lives on the line for them. To share the suffering of those treated unjustly.

Love Mercy

It's a wonderful word, "mercy"—if we're on the receiving end. We've all been in that situation. The police pull you over. You know you were going a little faster than you should. As the officer comes to the car window, you know you owe a fine. But what do you hope for? Perhaps just a warning ticket. You don't deserve it, but you hope for mercy.

Perhaps it's happened to you in a more personal and profound way. Every once in a while you wake up and see what kind of husband or wife you have been. Or what kind of father or mother or child. Sometimes we realize, "This is what they all have been putting up with all these years." We are struck by the level of mercy our own family has shown us.

Mercy is such a marvelous thing. We all love mercy. But loving mercy in this passage means more than loving to receive it. It means loving to show mercy to others. To give others not what they deserve but what we would want to receive if we were in their shoes.

The word here for mercy in Hebrew is one of the richest in that language. It is sometimes translated "grace" or "covenant loyalty." God has been faithful to his covenant with us by constantly forgiving us and showing us his grace. We are called to show the same mercy to others that God has shown to us.

That means we show mercy to those who do not deserve it. We are kind to the unkind. Loyal to the disloyal. God did not wait until we straightened out our act before he gave us mercy. He loved us while we were still sinners.

The New Testament puts it this way:

> We love because he first loved us. If anyone says, "I love God," yet hates his brother, he is a liar. For anyone who does not love his brother, whom he has seen, cannot love God, whom he has not seen. And he has given us this command: Whoever loves God must also love his brother.
> 1 John 4:19-21

Act justly. Love mercy. What does it take to meet God's requirements? It takes loving God. But loving God sounds much easier than loving people—real people, people I can see. People who don't always do things right. That is, they don't do them my way. Who don't always see things as clearly as I see them. People who lie about me. People who do all they can to harm me.

But that's what it means to love mercy.

Walk Humbly

What does God require? Bring in justice. Treat others with kindness, mercy, and love. And act a certain way toward God. Throughout the Bible, that way is called a walk. Who is the first person described as walking with God? "Enoch walked with God; then he was no more, because God took him away" (Genesis 5:24).

What does it mean to have a relationship with God? We walk. We sometimes sing about walking with God and Christ, hand in hand with Jesus. The word "walk" is chosen intentionally. Some of us are not always content to walk with God; we want to run with God. We want him to do things on our timetable. God is too slow for some of us. We won't wait for his pace.

Others of us may not want to walk at all. We want to let God carry us. Walking takes some effort, some patience. As Eugene Peterson says, walking is "a long obedience in the same direction." Walking with God is no Sunday stroll, but a lifelong journey of faith. It requires getting up each day and saying, "Today, I'm going to walk with God. I'm not going to guide my own footsteps, but let God guide me. I'm not going to worry about where I want to go or what I want to do. I'll let God tell me what he wants me to do and where he wants me to go."

We walk with God, but he leads. We follow.

"Walk humbly with your God." We dare not take God by the hand to lead him around. If we walk humbly, we won't even ask, "What does God require?" Walking humbly means we keep our focus on what he has done for us. He led us by the hand out of the slavery of sin.

We focus on who he wants us to be, not on our own dreams and ambitions. He wants us to treat others fairly and work to bring in a more just society. He wants us to show kindness and mercy to others who do not deserve it. He wants us, through every step and fork in the road, to make our decisions based on what he wills.

The Measure of a Life

I attend many funerals. Recently I was present at the funeral of a Christian named Mary. At a funeral, the question is always raised, "What made this person's life worthwhile?" Many avoid funerals because they remind us that we will someday have one of our own.

There the question will come, "What did our lives count for?"

How do you measure a life? Was Mary wealthy? No. Was she famous, did many people know her? No. Did she have a family? Yes. Was she part of God's family? Yes. Is that how you measure a life?

I think you measure her life this way: she was a woman who acted justly, who loved mercy, who walked humbly with her God.

When our time comes, whenever that may be, this will be the whole measure of our life. Not accomplishments or titles or how many knew us. Not even our family relationships, as important as they are. No, we will be measured by one thing. Are we God's people? Or perhaps by three. Did we do justice? Did we show God's kindness and love? Were we content to walk with our God?

In the words of Isaac Watts, "Love so amazing, so divine, demands my soul, my life, my all." That's what God requires. Or in the words of Jesus, "Follow me." In the light of the cross, his yoke is indeed easy, his burden light.

Radical Answers to Relevant Questions

What have we learned from these prophets who wrote so long ago? How can such old words be relevant to us? We've called their words radical answers in the literal sense of the word. "Radical" means going to the root of a problem. The true root or origin of the problem of contemporary life is our failure to remember what it means to be in relationship with the Eternal God. It was the same in the times of these prophets.

So, what are their answers? First, they tell us about the God we serve. He is a God who is faithful, even when we are faithless (Hosea). At times, he seems unfair to us, but he will remember his people and deliver them (Habakkuk). He is a God who is rightfully angry at evil (Nahum) but who will show mercy to anyone (Jonah). This is not just the God of these prophets. He is our God. A just God, rich in mercy.

The Minor Prophets also tell us who we are. Whether we are winners or mere survivors, God has chosen us to be his children (Obadiah). As such, he demands more from us (Amos). He wants us to reflect his character. To give generously because he is generous (Malachi). To do justice, love mercy, and walk humbly (Micah).

Thus our relationship with God is always shown in how we treat others. We constantly teach our children about this God of mercy (Joel). We reach our neighbors with good news (Zechariah) so God can cause our churches to grow (Haggai). We work, in God's name, to make our cities what they should be (Zephaniah).

The God of grace and mercy does not change; neither has the fallen world in which we live. God calls us today, as he called his people through these prophets, to be radically faithful to him in times of unfaithfulness. These prophets show us how.

Questions for Discussion

1. Do we ever find God's requirements burdensome? Is God a "picky" God, looking to trip us up on the fine print of his commands? Is he a God of the details?

2. Is it possible for Christians to personally be fair but to neglect justice on a larger scale? What responsibility do we have for justice in our government and our law

courts?

3. Who has harmed you the most in the last year? Have you shown mercy to them? How?

4. What does the word "walk" bring to your mind? Why is our relationship with God described as a walk?

5. What will be said about you at your funeral? What do you want said?

6. What is the most interesting or surprising thing you have learned from this study of the Minor Prophets?